CYRANO DE BERGERAC

CYRANO DE BERGERAC

BY
EDMOND ROSTAND

ILLUSTRATED BY
Nino Carbe

IN THE TRANSLATION BY
Helen B. Dole

NEW YORK
Illustrated Editions Company
100 FIFTH AVENUE

Printed in the United States of America by
J. J. LITTLE & IVES COMPANY NEW YORK

INTRODUCTION
AND
CRITICAL COMMENTARY

❧❧❧❧❧❧❧❧❧❧❧❧❧❧❧❧❧❧❧❧❧❧❧❧❧❧❧❧❧

Introduction

MANY who read this book will read it with a memory of the play as they have seen it. And such is the sweep of the play, so thrilling is Cyrano to the contemplation, that no reader or hearer will ask where or how. This world of the play is never-never land, where all things are possible, dazzling and marvellous things. But never-never land is fragile. It can be demolished by an incident, as when an amateur psychologist dismisses Cyrano with a shrug and remarks that the hero is after all only a neurotic, laboring under an inferiority complex resulting from facial disfigurement. Bah!

If Cyrano is a neurotic, take him as a fine model for a neurotic age. Pride and confidence he certainly has, in plenty enough to meet our needs with what spills over. If he is magnificent in never-never land, how much more is he magnificent in the tough and stormy Seventeenth Century.

Look at this: We are in a new country, a nation barely forty years old. Henry of Navarre brought it into being when he seized the French throne in 1589. He reigned for twenty years, and his nine-year-old son became Louis XIII. As this child grew up, Richelieu drew together the strings of the power he wielded till his death. Cyrano de Bergerac was born about 1619.

As the play opens, Paris is the capital of a revivified nation. The giants are young—Descartes is a man of forty-odd; Pascal is in his prime; Corneille has only recently abandoned comedies to write *Le Cid,* highly acclaimed in its first performance a few scant years back; Racine is a year-old baby; Molière is applying the perfecting touch to the vulgar old-time farces; Richelieu governs France, and the Academy is an innovation of but five years standing. Politics and government are tangled in an anarchy of obsolescent feudalism. Art and letters are no less helter-skelter; a swarm of dillettante literati has erected a mass of tasteless and inane conventions in a cancerous extravagance of imagination. Preciosity is the height of fashion, the current craze. The Renaissance, in short, is at its zenith in France, and in the midst of the intellectual and artistic excitement sound standards are overcoming outworn traditional practice and prettyfied triviality.

Into this capital of furious activity hurtles a headlong genius from Gascony. His personality seizes Paris—brains and unquenchable impudence in equal parts. He is nineteen, this walking gargoyle, and he endears friends and embitters enemies with every word he pronounces. The violent incandescence of life in him dazzles even a violent age. His sword-arm is a match for a hundred—no metaphor, this, but a solid fact of history. He flouts with equal verve nobility, clergy or reigning beauties—drives a ham actor from the stage under the cardinal's very eye, mocks foppish lordlings, and orders the *précieuses* in almost so many words to shut up and stay quiet. For fifteen years such things go on—no one can daunt him or hush him. He lets no chance escape to deride a fool or denounce a rascal. Some desperate victim, at last, ambushes him and drops a log of firewood on his head. And with the tumultuous fellow silenced at last, Paris catches its breath and tries to forget him for two centuries and a half. Then, in an age when the theater of Paris has narrowed its world to the space between perfumed bed sheets, Cyrano returns. Rostand presents him, Paris and the world goes wild—and sits back again to catch its breath. He is strenuous—too crushing and shocking in his impact on our thoughts and emotions, no companion for weaklings.

*   *   *   *

And now, for those who wish further to know Cyrano, here are a few dry-as-dust facts of history. His writings are preserved in old libraries, collected and published after his death by his friend Le Bret. There are modern editions and English translations of some. *L'histoire comique des états de la lune* and *L'histoire comique des états du soleil* are the easiest to locate. They contain, incidentally, forecasts of such things as Esperanto and phonographs. *Agrippine* and *Le pédant joué* are harder to find, and the writer knows of no place in the United States where the *Lettres* can be found nor *Le ministre d'état flambé*.

*   *   *   *

In the excitement of contemplating Cyrano, we forget text, scene and actor. Reading the play, we are apt to look neither above nor below the lines, not stopping to appraise or criticise. Though the author and translator will not resent this neglect or suffer from it, it would be unfair not to invite attention to the supreme deftness of Mrs. Dole's accomplishment in bringing Cyrano out of his own language into ours.

The high merit of the work is accentuated by adherence to one consistent viewpoint—that of the person who reads the play in printed form. For that reason she has chosen prose instead of verse, and we can rejoice who know that dramatic verse may be sweet to hear but is surely hard to read. For the same reason, she respects the untranslatable elements of the French; we are spared such an atrocity as *an intellectual* for *une précieuse,* and we are permitted to read *The Ballade of the Duel* and *The Cadets of Gascony* in their native melody and rhythm, with a literal translation to guide the understanding. If only other translators exercised equal restraint! Mrs. Dole's work deserves superlatives. The publisher could not have chosen a better piece of work from among the half-dozen efforts that have appeared since the first performance.

If the text of the play is of high quality, we can speak in the same terms of Nino Carbe's drawings. They radiate from the paper a vital essence comparable to Cyrano in the flesh. Mr. Carbe is a former pupil of Willy Pogany, and Mr. Pogany recommended him in these words: "He has all the gifts of imagination to do justice to such an eminent piece of literature. . . . He is an artist of great and *unlimited* ability."

*   *   *   *

And now, *voici les cadets de Gascogne.*

W. L. PARKER

New York,
October 1st, 1931

Critical Commentary

THE critic of literature has no more difficult task than that
of appraising properly a work that has achieved current success
to an eminent degree. Such a work needs no interpreter or
introducer, because it has already introduced itself. It does not
lend itself readily to calm judgment, both because the critic is
liable to be influenced by the same enthusiasm that has affected
the general public, and because, on the other hand, if he has
not been so influenced, he is likely to be overanxious to prove
his own independence, and is thus in danger of becoming
captious and unjust. Yet it is obvious that if there be any good
in criticism, successful authors, who presumably will become
still greater public benefactors, ought to get the benefit of it,
while the reader who is in danger of being misled by his enthusiasm should be set straight at once. Hence contemporary
criticism of all books, successful or unsuccessful, is practically
indispensable, and hence it is that even CYRANO DE BERGERAC,
fascinating though it be, cannot escape the common fate of
being weighed in the balance.

That it should have tipped the balance in both directions
since its production was to be expected. It was welcomed with a
warmth which probably neither its talented author, M. Edmond Rostand, nor its chief actor, M. Coquelin, fully antici-
pated; it was translated for foreign readers and adapted to
foreign stages; it was pronounced a masterpiece by critics of
established repute. But less flattering opinions were also heard.
Here in America, Norman Hapgood did not hesitate to declare
that the drama was to him "on the stage what it had been
in the reading,—an extremely clever proof of skill, a brilliant
show of execution, a series of scenes exactly calculated to

exhibit the powers of a strong and versatile French actor,—all this, but without simplicity, inevitableness, deep sincerity, without, in short, any true greatness." Mr. Stanley Young asserted that "not even Shakespeare has given us a hero that appeals to us as Cyrano," and that if we "search the whole range of Corneille, Racine, Molière, Victor Hugo, or any other French dramatist," we shall "find nothing on a higher level." Which of these two judgments is the correct one, or does not experience teach us rather that neither judgment is likely to be entirely correct and that we shall do well to seek a safe stand between them?

The important question is whether M. Rostand has succeeded in writing a great play. As we have seen, the public, everywhere, and a large number of critics think that he has. A few bold critics maintain that he has not, and a few readers, not so bold, discreetly hold their tongues. If numbers are to count in such a matter, M. Rostand's case is won—his play is the chief contribution to dramatic literature that has been made for many years.

Now, plainly, the opinion of the majority ought to count in such a matter, and just as plainly, the objections that can be raised against the drama should have a respectful hearing. But what are these objections? This question may be answered somewhat as follows:—

The play is called a "heroic comedy," yet it degenerates almost to opera bouffe in the fourth act, which also embraces a tragic element in the death of Christian, while the fifth act is filled with sentimental romance—the very last element a true comedy ought to contain. Again, Cyrano is the only character who is a distinct person, and one person with many personages cannot furnish sufficient play of character to equip a great comedy. Comedy there is in certain scenes,—as, for example, in the fifth scene of the third act, in which Christian fails so egregiously to make the proper sort of love to Roxane, —but the suggestion of romantic melodrama is never far removed. In other words, the play seems to be a good deal of a hybrid, to lack the essential unity of a true work of art. On the other hand, viewed merely as a piece of literature, it may be described with some reason as a clever rather than a truly witty or humorous performance, and as being fuller of charm than of compelling power. It amuses us and delights us, but it appeals to the fancy much more than to the imagination, and it furnishes us with little of that "criticism of life" which Matthew Arnold has taught us to demand from all poetry that challenges our admiration. This may, indeed, seem to be a rigorous test to apply to such a play, but after all CYRANO DE BERGERAC is a poetic drama, and its admirers have applied to it terms of praise hitherto confined to the world's few indisputable masterpieces.

It is now time, however, to consider some of the things that may be said in favor of the play. In the first place, it is certainly most effective. It interests spectator or reader, and fills him with a sympathy which purges him of selfishness and low emotions. It is impossible not to be drawn to Cyrano; we pity his misfortunes and admire his self-abnegation. Our critical judgment may tell us that M. Rostand is not the first dramatist to present his hero as an exemplar of almost superhuman self-sacrifice, but we must confess that he has on the whole succeeded remarkably well in the task he set himself. It may not have been a fit task for a comic dramatist, but its accomplishment at least shows distinguished power and an unusual comprehension of the demands of the theater-going public of the present day, which, weary of realism, has been glad to get back to romantic drama. The historical setting of the play is excellent, and the invention displayed in its construction is worthy of high praise. M. Rostand may not have given us enough of the higher side of the real Cyrano, he may have subordinated philosophy to sentiment, but surely no one save a born dramatist could have elaborated so effective a plot out of the scanty materials at hand. For it must be remembered that while many an episode and speech in the play must be credited to M. Rostand's researches, its central conception must be credited to his inventive genius. This central conception is effective even if not fully great: hence it seems hardly fair to accuse him of merely writing a clever series of scenes designed to bring out the talents of a great actor. He has done this, and he has yielded to the current demand for the spectacular far more than he should have done; but, with all his errors as an artist still in his prentice days, he has developed a character and produced a moving drama. And he is surely young enough to outgrow spectacular melodrama and such opera-bouffe tricks as the introduction of a "buffet-coach" on the stage.

But our author is more than an effective dramatist of great promise, he is also a genuine poet. His verses lack the depth and sincerity characteristic of the poetic drama at its height in the hands of Shakespeare or Sophocles; they have not the impetus that Victor Hugo gave to his; but they possess lyric charm to a marked degree. They are never flat, though perhaps never rarely beautiful; but it is at least certain that they are the work of an opulent artist. Passage after passage might be cited to prove the truth of this contention, but a few must suffice.

The famous line in the equally famous passage describing a kiss as—

"Un point rose qu'on met sur l'i du verbe aimer"

has been too much praised in all probability, as it is little more than cleverly pretty; but there is surely genuine poetry in these lines descriptive of Paris by moonlight:—

"Ah! . . . Paris fuit, nocturne et quasi nébuleux;
Le clair de lune coule aux pentes des toits bleus;
Un cadre se prépare, exquis, pour cette scène;
Là-bas, sous des vapeurs en écharpe, la Seine
Comme un mystérieux et magique miroir
Tremble. . . ."

18

An even more definite proof of M. Rostand's poetic ability is to be found in his melodious use of proper names. He does not rival Milton, but he deserves praise, in his own right, for lines like these:—

> "Mais . . . j'en vois plus d'un membre;
> Voici Boudu, Boissat, et Cureau de la Chambre,
> Porchères, Colomby, Bourzeys, Bourdon, Arbaud . . .
> Tous ces noms dont pas un ne mourra, que c'est beau."

Again, how well an old legend is handled in the following verses:—

> "La sage Pénélope
> Ne fût pas demeurée à broder sous son toit,
> Si le seigneur Ulysse eût écrit comme toi,
> Mais pour le joindre, elle eût, aussi folle qu'Hélène,
> Envoyé promener ses pelotons de laine!"

Finally, how concisely and inevitably the *motif* of the play is summed up in this couplet:—

> "Je vous dois d'avoir eu tout au moins une amie.
> Grâce à vous une robe a passé dans ma vie."

In view of these passages, and scores of others, it seems idle to deny that M. Rostand is one of the most skillful poets of our times. In view of the effectiveness of his drama, it is equally idle to deny that we have a right to look upon his play as an artistic event of international importance. For, whatever faults we may discover in CYRANO, we are surely somewhat blind if we do not discover in its author a remarkable affluence of power. Now affluence may be characteristic either of talents or of genius, and it would be rash to assert positively which sort of affluence M. Rostand possesses. But, after all, there are only a few affluent men born to a generation, and when the public recognizes one of them, it is surely within its rights when it greets him with acclamation. It may mistake talents, or even a single talent, for genius, but posterity can easily rectify the error, which is, at least, a generous one. Hence,

those of us who have admired M. Rostand's play have no need
to be ashamed to own our liking; and hence, too, any attempt,
like the present translation, to make the drama better known
outside of France, is to be heartily welcomed.

W. P. TRENT.

Dedication

I wished to dedicate this poem to CYRANO's *soul;*
But since it has passed into you, COQUELIN, *to you*
       I dedicate it.

                                        E. R.

DRAMATIS PERSONÆ

CYRANO DE BERGERAC.

CHRISTIAN DE NEUVILLETTE.

COMTE DE GUICHE.

RAGUENEAU.

LE BRET.

CAPTAIN CARBON DE CASTEL-
  JALOUX.

CADETS.

LIGNIERE.

DE VALVERT.

MONTFLEURY.

BELLEROSE.

JODELET.

CUIGY.

BRISSAILLE.

THREE MARQUISES.

A BORE.

TWO MUSKETEERS.

A SPANISH OFFICER.

A LIGHT-HORSEMAN.

THE DOORKEEPER.

A TRADESMAN.

HIS SON.

A PICKPOCKET.

A SPECTATOR.

A GUARD.

BERTRANDOU THE FIFER.

THE CAPUCHIN.

TWO MUSICIANS.

POETS.

PASTRY-COOKS.

ROXANE.

SISTER MARTHE.

LISE.

A REFRESHMENT GIRL.

MOTHER MARGUÉRITE DE JÉSUS.

THE DUENNA.

SISTER CLAIRE.

AN ACTRESS.

THE SOUBRETTE.

PAGES.

FLOWER-GIRL.

The Crowd, Tradesmen, Marquises, Musketeers, Pickpockets, Pastry-cooks, Poets, Gascony Cadets, Comedians, Musicians, Pages, Children, Spanish Soldiers, Spectators, Précieuses, Actresses, Nuns, etc.

(The first four acts in 1640, the fifth in 1655.)

CYRANO DE BERGERAC

ACT FIRST

A Performance at the Hôtel de Bourgogne.

The hall in the Hôtel de Bourgogne in 1640. A sort of tennis-court fitted up and decorated for theatrical performances.

The hall is oblong, seen diagonally in such a way that one of its sides forms the background which starts from the front wing on the right and goes to the farthest wing on the left, forming an angle with the stage, which is seen obliquely.

This stage is supplied with benches on both sides along the wings. The curtain is formed of two tapestries, which can be drawn apart. Above Harlequin's cloak, the royal arms. Broad steps lead from the stage into the hall. Place for violins on either side of these steps. Candles for footlights.

Two rows of galleries, one above the other along the sides; the upper row is divided into boxes. No seats in the pit, which is the stage of the theatre; at the back of this pit, that is to say on the right foreground, a few benches, and under a staircase leading to the upper seats, and of which only the beginning is to be seen, a sort of refreshment table decorated with cande-labra, vases of flowers, crystal glasses, plates of cakes, bottles, etc.

At the back of the stage, in the middle, under the gallery of boxes, the entrance to the theatre. A large door, opening part way to let in the spectators. On the door, as well as in several corners, and above the refreshment table, red posters announcing: "La Clorise."

When the curtain rises the hall is dimly lighted and empty. The chandeliers are lowered in the centre of the pit, ready to be illuminated.

〜〜〜〜〜〜〜〜〜〜〜〜〜〜〜〜〜〜

SCENE FIRST

The Audience *coming in a few at a time.* Cavaliers, Tradesman, Lackeys, Pages, a Pickpocket, a Doorkeeper, etc. *Then the* Marquises, CUIGY, BRISSAILLE, the Refreshment Girl, Musicians, etc.

(*Behind the door is heard a tumult of voices, then a* Cavalier *enters abruptly.*)

THE DOORKEEPER (*pursuing him*). Hold on! Your fifteen sous!

THE CAVALIER. I come in free!

THE DOORKEEPER. Why?

THE CAVALIER. I belong to the King's Cavalry!

DOORKEEPER (*to another Cavalier who has just entered*). You?

SECOND CAVALIER. I do not pay!

DOORKEEPER. But—

SECOND CAVALIER. I am a musketeer.

FIRST CAVALIER (*to the Second*). The play doesn't begin until two o'clock. The pit is empty. Let us try the foils.

(*They fence with the foils they have brought.*)

A LACKEY (*entering*). Pst—Flanquin!

ANOTHER (*who has already arrived*). Champagne?

THE FIRST (*showing him some cards which he draws out of his doublet*). Cards. Dice. (*He sits down on the ground.*) Let's play.

THE SECOND (*also sitting on the ground*). All right, you rascal.

FIRST LACKEY (*taking from his pocket a candle-end, which he lights and sticks into the ground*). I have abstracted a little light from my master.

A GUARD (*to a Flower-girl coming in*). It is fine to come before they light up!

(*Puts his arm around her waist.*)

ONE OF THE FENCERS (*struck with a foil*). Touch!

ONE OF THE CARD-PLAYERS. Clubs!

THE GUARD (*following the girl*). A kiss!

THE FLOWER-GIRL (*slipping away*). Some one will see us!

THE GUARD (*pulling her into a dark corner*). There's no danger!

A MAN (*seating himself on the ground with others who have brought eatables*). When one comes early, it is good to have something to eat.

A TRADESMAN (*accompanied by his son*). Let us sit here, my son.

A CARD-PLAYER. A pair of aces!

A MAN (*taking out a bottle from under his cloak, and sitting down also*). A toper should drink his bourgogne . . . (*he drinks*) in the Hôtel de Bourgogne!

THE TRADESMAN (*to his son*). Wouldn't you believe we are in some evil place? (*He points at the toper with the end of his cane*). Tipplers! (*As they fence one of the Cavaliers jostles him.*) Fighters! (*He falls between the Card-players.*) Gamblers!

THE GUARD (*behind him, still teasing the girl.*) A kiss!

THE TRADESMAN (*hastily drawing his son away*). Heavens! To think that in a hall like this they played Rotrou, my son!

THE YOUNG MAN. And Corneille!

A BAND OF PAGES (*hand in hand, enter dancing and singing*). Tra la la la la la la la la la la la.

THE DOORKEEPER (*severely, to the Pages*). Pages, no fooling!

FIRST PAGE (*with wounded dignity*). Oh, sir, what an idea! (*Quickly, to the Second, as soon as the Doorkeeper has turned his back.*) Have you some twine?

THE SECOND. With a fish-hook.

FIRST PAGE. From above there we could fish for somebody's wig.

A PICKPOCKET (*gathering around him several men of evil appearance*). You young swindlers, come and take a lesson: then you can practise thieving for the first time.

SECOND PAGE (*calling to other Pages already seated in the upper galleries*). Help! Have you some pea-shooters?

THIRD PAGE (*from above*). And peas too!

(*He blows and pelts them with peas.*)

THE YOUNG MAN (*to his father*). What is going to be played?

THE TRADESMAN. "Clorise."

THE YOUNG MAN. Whom is it by?

THE TRADESMAN. By Monsieur Balthazar Baro. It is a masterpiece!

(*He goes to the back of the pit on his son's arm.*)

THE PICKPOCKET (*to his acolytes*). Cut off the lace from the breeches.

A SPECTATOR (*to another, pointing to an upper corner*). See, at the first presentation of the "Cid," I was up there!

THE PICKPOCKET (*making gestures of spiriting things away*). The watches . . .

THE TRADESMAN (*returning with his son*). You will see some very celebrated actors.

THE PICKPOCKET (*making sly, little gestures of picking a pocket*). Handkerchiefs . . .

THE TRADESMAN. Montfleury.

SOME ONE (*calling from the upper gallery*). Light the lights!

THE TRADESMAN. Bellerose, l'Épy, la Beaupré, Jodelet!

A PAGE (*in the pit*). Ah! here comes the refreshment girl!

THE REFRESHMENT GIRL (*appearing behind the refreshment stand*). Oranges, milk, raspberry shrub, lemonade.

(*Uproar at the door.*)

A FALSETTO VOICE. Make room, brutes!

A LACKEY (*in surprise*). Marquises! . . . in the pit?

ANOTHER LACKEY. Oh, only for a few minutes.

(*Enter a band of foppish Marquises.*)

A MARQUIS (*seeing the hall half empty*). What! Do we come in like drapers, without disturbing people? without stepping on their toes? Oh, fie! fie! fie! (*He finds himself among other noblemen, who have come in a little before.*) Cuigy! Brissaille! (*Grand embracing.*)

CUIGY. Ye faithful! Yes, we have come before the candles are lighted.

THE MARQUIS. Oh, don't speak about it! I am in a humor—

ANOTHER. Console yourself, Marquis, for here is the lamplighter!

THE AUDIENCE (*greeting the lamplighter*). Ah!

(*The people gather around the chandeliers which he is lighting. Some have taken seats in the galleries.* LIGNIÈRE *enters the pit, giving his arm to* CHRISTIAN DE NEUVILLETTE. LIGNIÈRE *rather carelessly dressed, with the face of a notorious toper.* CHRISTIAN *elegantly attired, but in a style somewhat behind the times, seems preoccupied and fixes his attention on the boxes.*)

SCENE SECOND

The Same, CHRISTIAN, LIGNIÈRE, *then* RAGUENEAU, *and* LE BRET

CUIGY. Lignière!

BRISSAILLE (*laughing*). Not yet tipsy?

LIGNIÈRE (*in a low voice to Christian*). Shall I present you? (*Sign of assent from Christian.*) Baron de Neuvillette. (*Bows.*)

THE AUDIENCE (*applauding the rise of the first lighted chandelier*). Ah!

CUIGY (*to Brissaille, while looking at Christian*). He has a charming head.

FIRST MARQUIS (*who has overheard*). Pooh!

LIGNIÈRE (*presenting to Christian*). Messieurs de Cuigy, de Brissaille.

CHRISTIAN (*bowing*). Delighted!

FIRST MARQUIS (*to Second*). He is handsome enough, but he is not dressed in style.

LIGNIÈRE (*to Cuigy*). He has just come from Touraine.

CHRISTIAN. Yes, I have hardly been in Paris twenty days. I enter the guards tomorrow, the Cadets.

FIRST MARQUIS (*looking at the people as they enter the boxes*). There is President Aubrey's wife!

THE REFRESHMENT GIRL. Oranges, milk . . .

THE VIOLINS (*tuning up*).

CUIGY (*to Christian, calling his attention to the fact that the hall is filling up*). How many people there are!

CHRISTIAN. Ah, yes, a great many.

FIRST MARQUIS. All the fashionable world!

(*They name the women as, elegantly dressed, they enter the boxes. Exchange of bows and smiles.*)

SECOND MARQUIS. Mesdames de Guéménée . . .

CUIGY. De Bois-Dauphin.

FIRST MARQUIS. Whom we were in love with.

BRISSAILLE. De Chavigny.

SECOND MARQUIS. Who plays with our hearts!

LIGNIÈRE. By the way, Monsieur de Corneille has returned from Rouen!

THE YOUNG MAN (*to his father*). Is the Academy represented there?

THE TRADESMAN. Yes—I see more than one member; there is Boudu, Boissat, and Cureau de la Chambre, Porchères, Colomby, Bourzeys, Bourdon, Arbaud—all these names not one of which will die, how fine a thing it is!

FIRST MARQUIS. Attention! Our *précieuses* are taking their seats: Barthénoïde, Urimédonte, Cassandace, Felixérie . . .

SECOND MARQUIS. Gracious! Their names are charming! Do you know them all, Marquis?

FIRST MARQUIS. I know them all, Marquis!

LIGNIÈRE (*taking Christian aside*). My dear, I have come to do you a favor: the lady does not come. I return to my sins!

CHRISTIAN (*beseechingly*). No! You who sing of the city and the court, stay: you will tell me for whom I am dying of love.

THE FIRST VIOLIN (*striking his desk with his bow*). Gentlemen.

(*He raises his bow.*)

THE REFRESHMENT GIRL. Macaroons lemonade . . .

(*The violins begin to play.*)

CHRISTIAN. I fear she is a coquette and clever.
I dare not speak to her for I have no wit.
The language of to-day as it is spoken and written perplexes me. I am only a good soldier, lacking courage. She is always on the right, at the back, in yonder empty box.

LIGNIÈRE (*starting to go out*). I am going.

CHRISTIAN (*detaining him*). Oh, no, stay!

LIGNIÈRE. I cannot. D'Assoucy is waiting for me at the wine-shop. I should die of thirst, here.

THE REFRESHMENT GIRL (*passing in front of him with a tray*). Sherbet?

LIGNIÈRE. Fie!

THE REFRESHMENT GIRL. Milk?

LIGNIÈRE. Pooh!

THE REFRESHMENT GIRL. Muscat?

LIGNIÈRE. Hold on! (*To Christian*). I will stay a little longer. Let us see this Muscat.

(*He seats himself near the refreshment stand. The girl pours out some Muscat for him.*)

THE AUDIENCE (*exclaims at the entrance of a fat, jolly little man.*) Ah! Ragueneau!

LIGNIÈRE (*to Christian*). The great pastry-cook, Ragueneau.

RAGUENEAU (*in the Sunday costume of a pastry-cook, quickly approaching Lignière.*) Sir, have you seen Monsieur Cyrano?

LIGNIÈRE (*presenting Ragueneau to Christian*). The pastry-cook of actors and of poets!

RAGUENEAU (*in confusion*). Too much honor.

LIGNIÈRE. Hold your tongue, Mæcenas that you are!

RAGUENEAU. Yes, these gentlemen patronize me . . .

LIGNIÈRE. On credit. He is a poet of talent himself—

RAGUENEAU. They tell me so.

LIGNIÈRE. Crazy over poetry!

RAGUENEAU. It is true that for an odelet—

LIGNIÈRE. You give a tart.

RAGUENEAU. Oh! a tartlet!

LIGNIÈRE. The worthy man makes his excuse! And for a triolet what do you give?

RAGUENEAU. Rolls!

LIGNIÈRE (*severely*). Milk rolls. And you love the theatre?

RAGUENEAU. I adore it.

LIGNIÈRE. You pay for your theatre tickets in cakes! Your seat to-day, let's see, between us, cost you how much?

RAGUENEAU. Four custards. Fifteen puffs. (*He looks all around.*) Monsieur de Cyrano is not here? I am surprised.

LIGNIÈRE. Why?

RAGUENEAU. Montfleury plays!

LIGNIÈRE. To be sure, that hogshead is going to play the rôle of Phédon to-night. What is that to Cyrano?

RAGUENEAU. Why, don't you know? He has forbidden Montfleury, whom he detests, to appear on the stage again for a month.

LIGNIÈRE (*who is taking his fourth glass*). Well?

RAGUENEAU. Montfleury plays to-night!

CUIGY (*who had drawn near with his friends*). He can do nothing.

RAGUENEAU. Oh! oh! that is what I have come to see!

FIRST MARQUIS. Who is this Cyrano?

CUIGY. He is a fellow skilled in using the rapier.

SECOND MARQUIS. Noble?

CUIGY. Quite so. He is a Cadet in the Guards. (*Pointing to a gentleman walking to and fro in the audience as if looking for some one.*) But his friend Le Bret can tell you. (*He calls.*) Le Bret! (*Le Bret comes toward them.*) Are you looking for Bergerac?

LE BRET. Yes. I am anxious!

CUIGY. Isn't this man one of the most extraordinary?

LE BRET (*affectionately*). Ah! he is the most exquisite of sublunary beings!

RAGUENEAU. Rhymester!

CUIGY. Fighter!

BRISSAILLE. Physician.

LE BRET. Musician!

LIGNIÈRE. And what a heteroclitish appearance he has!

RAGUENEAU. Surely, I do not think that the solemn Sir Philippe de Champaigne will ever fight him for us; but strange, excessive, extravagant, ludicrous, as he is, he would have furnished, I think, to the late Jacques Callot, the maddest bully to place among his masques. In his hat with its triple plume, doublet with half a dozen skirts, and a cloak which the point of his sword lifts pompously behind, like a cock's insolent tail, prouder than all the Artabans to whom Gascony has been and always will be a fond Mother Gigogne, he sports in his Punchinello ruff a nose! Oh, gentlemen, what a nose it is! One cannot see such a proboscis without exclaiming, "Oh, no, truly, it's an exaggeration!" Then one smiles and says, "He will take it off." But Monsieur de Bergerac never takes it off.

LE BRET (*tossing his head*). He wears it,—and woe to him who ever remarks upon it!

RAGUENEAU (*proudly*). His blade is half the shears of Fate!

FIRST MARQUIS (*shrugging his shoulders*). He will not come!

RAGUENEAU. He will! I wager a chicken à la Ragueneau!

THE MARQUIS (*laughing*). Agreed!

(*Murmurs of admiration in the hall.* ROXANE *has just appeared in her box. She seats herself in front, her duenna takes a place at the back.* CHRISTIAN, *busy in paying the* Refreshment Girl, *does not see her.*)

SECOND MARQUIS (*exclaiming*). Ah! gentlemen! isn't she awfully charming?

FIRST MARQUIS. A peach with a strawberry smile.

SECOND MARQUIS. And so fresh that you might take cold in your heart if you came near her!

CHRISTIAN (*raises his head, sees Roxane, and quickly seizes Lignière's arm*). There she is!

LIGNIÈRE (*looking*). Ah! is she the one?

CHRISTIAN. Yes, tell me quickly. I am afraid.

LIGNIÈRE (*sipping his Muscat*). Magdeleine Robin, called Roxane. Bright. *Précieuse.*

CHRISTIAN. Alas!

LIGNIÈRE. Free. Orphan. A cousin to Cyrano—of whom they were just speaking.

(*At this moment, a very elegant lord, wearing the order of the Holy Ghost over his shoulder, enters the box, and standing, talks for a moment with* ROXANE.)

CHRISTIAN (*starting*). Who is that man?

LIGNIÈRE (*beginning to be tipsy, winking his eye*). He! He! Count de Guiche. In love with her. But married to the niece of Armand de Richelieu. Desirous of marrying Roxane to a certain sorry lord, Monsieur de Valvert, a viscount—and willing. She doesn't agree to it, but De Guiche is powerful; he knows how to persecute a simple girl. Besides I have exposed his crafty design in a song which—Ho! He ought to bear me a grudge!—The ending was malicious.—Listen.

(*He rises staggering, lifting his glass, ready to sing.*)

CHRISTIAN. No. Good night.

LIGNIÈRE. Are you going?

CHRISTIAN. To Monsieur de Valvert's!

LIGNIÈRE. Take care, he will kill you! (*Designating Roxane with the corner of his eye.*) Stay. You are observed.

CHRISTIAN. That is true!

(*He remains wrapt in thought. The group of pickpockets, at this moment noticing his head in the air and mouth open, approach him.*)

LIGNIÈRE. I am the one who is going. I am thirsty. I am expected at the wine-shops.

(*He goes out, reeling.*)

LE BRET (*who has been all around the hall, coming back to Ragueneau, in a tone of assurance*). No Cyrano.

RAGUENEAU (*incredulously*). However—

LE BRET. Ah! I should hope he has not seen the play-bill!

THE AUDIENCE. Begin! Begin!

SCENE THIRD

The Same, except LIGNIÈRE; DE GUICHE, VALVERT, *then* MONT-
FLEURY

A MARQUIS (*seeing De Guiche coming out of Roxane's box,
crossing the pit, surrounded by obsequious lords, the Viscount
de Valvert among them*). What a court has this De Guiche!

ANOTHER. Ff! Another Gascon!

THE FIRST. A cold, versatile Gascon, one who will succeed!
Believe me, we should pay our respects.

(*They go toward* DE GUICHE.)

SECOND MARQUIS. What fine ribbons! What is their color,
Count de Guiche? *Kiss-me-my-darling,* or *Breast-of-the-roe?*

DE GUICHE. This color is *Sick Spaniard.*

FIRST MARQUIS. The color does not lie, for soon, thanks to
your valor, the Spaniard will be sick in Flanders!

DE GUICHE. I am going on the stage. Will you come? (*Followed by all the Marquises and noblemen he makes his way
toward the theatre. He turns around and calls.*) Come, Valvert!

CHRISTIAN (*who is listening and watching them, starts at the
sound of this name*). The Viscount! Ah! I will throw in his
face my— (*He puts his hand in his pocket, and comes in con-
tact with that of a Pickpocket in the act of robbing him. He
turns around.*) What?

THE PICKPOCKET. Ay!

CHRISTIAN (*without letting him go*). I was looking for a
glove!

THE PICKPOCKET (*with a pitiful smile*). You find a hand.
(*Changing his tone, speaking low and quickly.*) Let me go!
I will tell you a secret.

34

CHRISTIAN (*still keeping hold of him*). What?

THE PICKPOCKET. Lignière—who has just left you—

CHRISTIAN (*the same action*). Ah! Well?

THE PICKPOCKET. —is near his last hour. A song that he made has offended some great person, and a hundred men—I am one of them—will be on the watch to-night!

CHRISTIAN. A hundred! By whom?

THE PICKPOCKET. A secret—

CHRISTIAN (*shrugging his shoulders*). Oh!

THE PICKPOCKET (*with much dignity*). Professional!

CHRISTIAN. Where will they be stationed?

THE PICKPOCKET. At the Porte de Nesle. On his path. Warn him!

CHRISTIAN (*at last releasing his wrist*). But where can I see him?

THE PICKPOCKET. Run to all the wine-shops: the Golden Wine-press, the Pine-apple, the Broken Girdle, the Two Torches, and the Three Funnels,—and in each leave a little note to warn him.

CHRISTIAN. Yes, I will go! Oh, the rascals! A hundred against a single man! (*Looking affectionately toward Roxane.*) To leave her—her! (*Angrily toward Valvert.*) And he!— But I must save Lignière!

(*He runs out.* DE GUICHE, *the* Viscount, *the* Marquises, *all the lords, have disappeared behind the curtain, to take their seats on the benches on the stage. The pit is entirely full. Not a seat vacant in the galleries and boxes.*)

THE AUDIENCE. Begin!

A TRADESMAN (*whose wig flies off on the end of a string, fished off by a Page in the upper gallery*). My wig!

EXCLAMATIONS OF AMUSEMENT. He is bald! Bravo, pages! Ha! ha! ha!

THE TRADESMAN (*furious, shaking his fist*). Little scamp!

LAUGHTER AND SHOUTS (*beginning very loud, and dying away*). Ha! ha! ha! ha! ha! ha!

(*Complete silence.*)

LE BRET (*in surprise*). Why this sudden silence? (*One of the spectators speaks to him in a low voice.*) Ah?

THE SPECTATOR. I have it on the very best authority.

MURMURS (*spreading through the audience*). Hush— Is he coming?—No!—Yes!—In the close box.—The Cardinal!—The Cardinal!—The Cardinal!

A PAGE. Oh! the devil, now there'll be no sport!

(*A knocking is heard on the stage. Everybody is motionless, in expectation.*)

THE VOICE OF A MARQUIS (*in the silence, behind the curtain*). Snuff that candle.

ANOTHER MARQUIS (*passing his head through the division in the curtain.*) A chair!

(*A chair is passed from hand to hand above the heads of the people. The Marquis takes it and disappears, after kissing his hand to the boxes.*)

A SPECTATOR. Silence!

(*Three knocks are heard again. The curtain opens. Tableau. The Marquises seated on the sides, in saucy attitudes. Back-scene representing a bluish-colored, pastoral landscape. Four little crystal chandeliers light the stage. The violins play softly.*)

LE BRET (*to Ragueneau, in an undertone*). Is Montfleury coming on the stage?

RAGUENEAU (*in an undertone also*). Yes, he has to begin.

LE BRET. Cyrano is not there.

RAGUENEAU. I have lost my wager.

LE BRET. All the better! all the better!

(*A bagpipe is heard, and* MONTFLEURY *appears on the stage. He is enormous, dressed in a pastoral shepherd's costume, his rose-trimmed hat worn over one ear, and he is blowing a be-ribboned bagpipe.*)

THE PIT (*applauding*). Bravo, Montfleury! Montfleury!

MONTFLEURY (*after bowing, playing the part of* PHÉDON).
"How happy he who far from courts alone
A voluntary exile to the woods has flown.
And who when Zephyr o'er the trees has blown——"

A VOICE (*from the middle of the pit*). Rascal, didn't I forbid it for a month?

(*Everybody, dumfounded, turns around. Murmurs.*)

DIFFERENT VOICES. Eh?—What?—What is it?

(*People in the boxes rise to see.*)

CUIGY. It is he!

LE BRET (*terrified*). Cyrano!

THE VOICE. King of buffoons, off the stage at once!

THE ENTIRE AUDIENCE (*indignant*). Oh!

MONTFLEURY. But—

THE VOICE. Do you persist?

DIFFERENT VOICES (*from the pit and the boxes*). Hush!—Enough—Montfleury, play!—Don't be afraid!

MONTFLEURY (*in a hesitating voice*). "How happy he who far from courts alone—"

THE VOICE (*more threatening*). Well? Must I plant a wood on your shoulders, oh monarch of knaves?

(*A cane at the end of an arm strikes out above the heads of the audience.*)

MONTFLEURY (*in a voice growing fainter and fainter*). "How happy he who—"

(*The cane is flourished.*)

THE VOICE. Leave!

THE PIT. Oh!

MONTFLEURY (*choking*). "How happy he who far from courts—"

CYRANO (*rising from the pit, standing on a chair, with folded arms, his hat cocked on one side, his mustache bristling, his nose terrible*). Ah! I shall be angry!

(*Sensation at sight of him.*)

SCENE FOURTH

The Same, CYRANO, *then* BELLEROSE, JODELET

MONTFLEURY (*to the Marquises*). Come to my aid, gentlemen!

A MARQUIS (*indifferently*). Well, play, then!

CYRANO. You big fellow, if you play, I shall be obliged to slap your face!

THE MARQUIS. Enough!

CYRANO. Let the Marquises be silent in their seats, or their ribbons will feel my cane!

ALL THE MARQUISES (*standing*). This is too much!—Montfleury—

CYRANO. Let Montfleury go, or I will cut off his ears and rip him open!

A VOICE. But—

CYRANO. Let him go!

ANOTHER VOICE. And yet?

CYRANO. Hasn't he gone yet? (*Turning up his sleeves.*) Good! I am going to the stage as if it were a sideboard to cut up this Italian sausage!

MONTFLEURY (*collecting all his dignity*). When you insult me, sir, you insult Thalia!

CYRANO (*very politely*). If this Muse to whom, sir, you are nothing, had the honor of your acquaintance, believe me, when she saw you as fat and stupid as an urn, she would lay her buskin on you soundly.

THE PIT. Montfleury!—Montfleury!—Give us Baro's play!

CYRANO (*to those who are shouting around him*). Have pity on my scabbard; if you go on, it will give up its blade!

(*The circle enlarges.*)

THE CROWD (*drawing back*). Take care! There!

CYRANO (*to Montfleury*). Leave the stage!

THE CROWD (*approaching and grumbling*). Oh! oh!

CYRANO (*turning around suddenly*). Does any one object?
(*They draw back again.*)

A VOICE (*singing at the back*).

> Monsieur de Cyrano,
> This tyranny must cease.
> Despite the blade you show,
> They *shall* play "La Clorise."

THE ENTIRE AUDIENCE (*singing*). La Clorise, La Clorise!

CYRANO. If I hear that song once more I will knock you down, every one of you.

A TRADESMAN. You are not Samson!

CYRANO. Will you lend me your jaw, sir?

A LADY (*in one of the boxes*). This is unheard of!

A NOBLEMAN. It is scandalous!

A TRADESMAN. It is vexatious!

A PAGE. What a waste of time!

THE PIT. Kss!—Montfleury!—Cyrano!

CYRANO. Silence!

THE PIT (*in a frenzy*). He-haw! Baa! Bow-wow! Cock-a-doodle-doo!

CYRANO. I command you—

A PAGE. Miaou!

CYRANO. I command you to be silent! And I challenge the pit collectively! I will write down your names! Draw near, young heroes! Each in his turn! I am going to number you! Come, who will open the list? You, sir? No! You? No! I will despatch the first duellist with all the honors due him! Let all who wish to die raise their finger! (*Silence.*) Does modesty forbid you from looking on my naked blade? Not one name? Not one finger? Very good. I will go on. (*Turning toward the stage where Montfleury is waiting in agony.*) Then, I desire to see the theatre cured of this swelling. If not—(*his hand on his sword*) the scalpel!

MONTFLEURY. I—

CYRANO (*gets down from the chair, seats himself in the middle of the circle formed around him, and makes himself at home*). I am going to clap three times, you full moon! At the third you will be eclipsed.

THE PIT (*amused*). Ah!

CYRANO (*clapping his hands*). One!

MONTFLEURY. I—

A VOICE (*from the boxes*). Stay!

THE PIT. He will stay.—He will not stay.—

MONTFLEURY. I believe, gentlemen—

CYRANO. Two!

MONTFLEURY. I am sure that it would be better—

CYRANO. Three!

(MONTFLEURY *disappears, as if through a trap-door. Tempest of laughter, whistles, and hoots.*)

THE AUDIENCE. Coward! Come back!

CYRANO (*beaming, throws himself back into his chair and crosses his legs*). Let him come back, if he dares!

A TRADESMAN. The orator of the troop!

(BELLEROSE *comes forward and bows.*)

THE BOXES. Ah! There is Bellerose!

BELLEROSE (*elegantly*). Noble Lords—

THE PIT. No! No! Jodelet!

JODELET (*comes forward, and speaking through his nose*). Pack of calves!

THE PIT. Ah! Ah! Bravo! Very good! Bravo!

JODELET. No bravos! The big tragedian whose paunch you take delight in has felt—

THE PIT. He's a coward!

JODELET. He was obliged to leave!

THE PIT. Let him come back!

SOME OF THEM. No!

OTHERS. Yes!

A YOUNG MAN (*to Cyrano*). But really, sir, what reason have you to hate Montfleury?

CYRANO (*graciously, still seated*). Young gosling, I have two reasons, either of which is sufficient alone. Primo: He is a wretched actor, who bawls and grunts like a water-carrier, over the verses that he ought to let soar away on wings! Secundo: That is my secret.

THE OLD TRADESMAN (*behind him*). But you are depriving us unscrupulously of "La Clorise"! I object!

CYRANO (*turning his chair toward the Tradesman, respectfully*). You donkey, old Baro's verses are worth less than nothing. I have no scruples in interrupting them!

THE PRÉCIEUSES (*in the boxes*). Ah! Oh! Our Baro! My dear! Is it possible? Oh Heavens!

CYRANO (*turning his chair toward the boxes, courteously*). Lovely ladies, shine, bloom, be the cup-bearers of our dreams, with a smile make death enchanting, inspire us to write verses —but do not criticise them!

BELLEROSE. But the money that must be given back!

CYRANO (*turning his chair to the stage*). Bellerose, you have made the only intelligent remark! I make no holes in the cloak of Thespis. (*He rises and throws a bag on the stage.*) Catch this purse on the fly and hold your tongue!

THE AUDIENCE (*dazzled*). Ah! Oh!

JODELET (*hastily picking up the purse and weighing it in his hand*). At this price, sir, I authorize you to come every day to stop "La Clorise."

THE AUDIENCE. Hoo! Hoo!

JODELET. We should all be hooted together!

BELLEROSE. The hall must be vacated!

JODELET. Clear it!

(*The people begin to go out, while* CYRANO *looks on with an air of satisfaction. But the crowd soon stops on hearing the following scene, and the going out ceases. The women in the boxes who were standing up with their cloaks on, stop to listen and finally sit down again.*)

LE BRET (*to Cyrano*). It's madness!

A BORE (*who has approached Cyrano*). The actor Montfleury! How scandalous! But he is protected by the Duke de Candale! Have you a patron?

CYRANO. No!

THE BORE. You have not?

CYRANO. No!

THE BORE. What, no great nobleman to protect you with his name?

CYRANO (*irritated*). No, I have told you so twice. Must I say it thrice? No, no protector (*his hand on his sword*), but a protectress!

THE BORE. But are you going to leave town?

CYRANO. That depends.

THE BORE. The Duke de Candale has a long arm!

CYRANO. Not so long as mine (*pointing to his sword*) when lengthened by this!

THE BORE. But you do not dream of pretending—

CYRANO. I do dream of it.

THE BORE. But—

CYRANO. Now start your boots.

THE BORE. But—

CYRANO. Start! Or tell me why you are looking at my nose.

THE BORE (*bewildered*). I—

CYRANO (*going toward him.*) What is there surprising about it?

THE BORE (*drawing back*). Your grace is mistaken—

CYRANO. Is it flabby and swaying like a trunk?

THE BORE (*drawing back again*). I did not—

CYRANO. Or hooked like an owl's beak?

THE BORE. I—

CYRANO. Do you notice a wart on the end of it?

THE BORE. But—

CYRANO. Or a fly slowly taking a walk over it? What is there so uncommon about it?

THE BORE. Oh!

CYRANO. Is it a phenomenon?

THE BORE. But I knew how to keep my eyes from it!

CYRANO. And why, if you please, should you keep your eyes from it?

THE BORE. I had—

CYRANO. Then you find it disgusting?

THE BORE. Sir!

CYRANO. Does its color seem unwholesome to you?

THE BORE. Sir!

CYRANO. Its shape obscene?

THE BORE. Not at all!

CYRANO. Why, then, do you put on such a sneering air? Perhaps you find it a little too large?

THE BORE (*stammering*). I find it small, very small—minute!

CYRANO. Eh! What! You accuse me of being so ridiculous? My nose small?

THE BORE. Heavens!

CYRANO. My nose is enormous! Mean flat-nose, stupid snub-nose! Dullard, I would have you know that I pride myself on such an appendage, inasmuch as a big nose is, properly speaking, the sign of an affable, kind, courteous, witty, liberal, courageous man, such as I am, and such as you can never think of being, miserable rascal! for the inglorious face that my hand is going to seek above your collar, is as bare—

(*He slaps his face.*)

THE BORE. Ow!

CYRANO. Of pride, of inspiration, of lyricism, of picturesqueness, of sparkle, of sumptuosity, of even a nose, as that (*he turns him around by the shoulders, suiting the action to the word*) which my boot is going to seek below your back!

THE BORE (*escaping*). Help! Guard!

CYRANO. Let this be a warning to the boobies, who might find the middle of my face amusing, and if the jester is of noble birth, my treatment is, before letting him escape, to apply the steel instead of leather, in front and higher up!

DE GUICHE (*who has come down from the stage, with the Marquises*). At last he grows tiresome!

THE VISCOUNT DE VALVERT (*shrugging his shoulders*). He is boastful!

DE GUICHE. Is no one going to reply to him?

THE VISCOUNT. No one? Wait! I am going to shoot an arrow

at him! (*He approaches Cyrano, who is watching him, and placing himself in front of him with a foppish air.*) You—you have a very—ah—a very—large nose.

CYRANO (*gravely*). Very.

THE VISCOUNT (*laughing*). Ha!

CYRANO (*unmoved*). Is that all?

THE VISCOUNT. But—

CYRANO. Ah! no! That is a little short, young man! One might make—oh, my Lord! many remarks, on the whole, by varying the tone, for example; listen:—

Aggressive: "Sir, if I had such a nose, I should have it amputated at once!"

Friendly: "It must dip into your cup: in order to drink you must have a goblet made for you!"

Descriptive: "It is a rock! It is a peak! It is a cape! What did I say? A cape? It is a peninsula!"

Curious: "For what do you use that oblong capsule? For an inkstand or a scissors-case?"

Gracious: "Do you love the birds so well that you take fatherly interest in holding out that perch for their little feet?"

Savage: "When you enjoy your pipe, sir, does the smoke ever come out of your nose without some neighbor crying that the chimney is on fire?"

Warning: "With such a weight dragging on your head, take care that you do not fall forward on the ground!"

Tender: "Have a little parasol made for it, for fear its color might fade in the sun!"

Pedantic: "Only the animal, sir, called by Aristophanes the Hippocampelephantocamelos, could have had so much flesh and bone under its forehead!"

Flippant: "What, my friend, is this hook in style? To hang one's hat on, it is surely very convenient!"

Emphatic: "No wind, except the mistral, could make you catch cold entirely, O magisterial nose!"

Dramatic: "When it bleeds it is the Red Sea!"

Admiring: "What a sign for a perfumer!"

Lyrical: "Is it a conch? Are you a triton?"

Naïve: "When can this monument be visited?"

Respectful: "Allow me, sir, to salute you: that is what is called having a house of one's own!"

Rustic: "Hallo, there! Is that a nose? It is a giant turnip or a dwarf melon!"

Military: "Point against the cavalry!"

Practical: "Will you put it in a lottery? Surely, sir, it will win the first prize."

Finally taking off Pyramus, with a sob: "There is that nose which has destroyed the harmony of its master's features! It makes him blush, the traitor!"

That is very nearly, my dear, what you would have said to me if you had a little knowledge of letters, and a little wit: but of wit, O most lamentable of beings, you never had an atom and of letters, you have only the four which form the word: Fool! Moreover, if you had had the invention necessary to make it possible for you, before these noble galleries, to serve me with all these mad pleasantries, you would not have uttered the quarter of the half of the beginning of one, because I serve them out to myself with enthusiasm, but I allow no one else to serve them to me.

DE GUICHE (*trying to lead away the petrified Viscount*). Viscount, what nonsense!

THE VISCOUNT (*suffocated*). Such grand arrogant airs! A country bumpkin, who—who—doesn't even wear gloves! And who goes out without ribbons, without bows, and without frogs.

CYRANO. I keep my elegance to adorn my morals. I do not deck myself out like a coxcomb, but I am more careful, if I am less vain. I would not go out through neglect, leaving an insult not washed away, with my conscience still yellow from sleep in the corner of its eye, my honor crumpled, my scruples in mourning. But I walk along with nothing upon me that does not shine, plumed with independence and sincerity; it is not a fine figure, it is my soul that I restrain as in a corset, and all covered with exploits, fastened on like ribbons, curling my wit like a mustache, as I pass through the crowd I make truths ring like spurs.

THE VISCOUNT. But, sir—

CYRANO. I have no gloves?—A serious matter! I have just one remaining of a very old pair! Which was once very troublesome to me. I threw it in some one's face.

THE VISCOUNT. Knave, rascal, ridiculous flat-footed clown.

CYRANO (*taking off his hat and bowing as if the Viscount had just introduced himself*). Ah? And I am Cyrano-Savinien-Hercule-de-Bergerac.

(*Laughter.*)

THE VISCOUNT (*exasperated*). Buffoon!

CYRANO (*crying out as if seized with the cramp*). Ay!—

THE VISCOUNT (*who was moving away, turning around*). Did he say something more?

CYRANO (*making up faces as if in pain*). It must be exercised or it will grow numb. This comes of leaving it idle!—

THE VISCOUNT. What is the matter?

CYRANO. I have a tingling in my sword!

THE VISCOUNT (*drawing his own*). So be it!

CYRANO. I will give you a charming little thrust.

THE VISCOUNT (*scornfully*). Poet!

CYRANO. Yes, sir, poet! and such an one that while fencing I am going to compose you a ballad, improvising.

THE VISCOUNT. A ballad?

CYRANO. You know what that is, I suppose?

THE VISCOUNT. But—

CYRANO (*as if reciting a lesson*). The ballad is composed of three stanzas, of eight lines—

THE VISCOUNT (*stamping*). Oh!

CYRANO (*continuing*). And of an envoi of four.

THE VISCOUNT. You—

CYRANO. I am going to compose one and fight you at the same time, and hit you, sir, at the last line.

THE VISCOUNT. No!

CYRANO. No? (*Declaiming.*) "Ballad of the duel which Monsieur de Bergerac fought with a rascal in the Hôtel de Bourgogne!"

THE VISCOUNT. What is the meaning of that, if you please?

CYRANO. That is the title.

THE AUDIENCE (*excited to the highest pitch*). Make room! Very amusing! Clear the way! No noise!

(Tableau. *Circle of curious spectators in the pit, the* Marquises *and* Officers *mingling with the tradesmen and common people;* Pages *climb on one another's shoulders to get a better view. All the women standing in the boxes. On the right,* DE GUICHE *and his noble friends. Left,* LE BRET, RAGUENEAU, CUIGY, *etc.*)

CYRANO (*closing his eyes for a second*). Wait! I am choosing my rhymes. There, I am ready.

CYRANO (*suiting the action to the words*).

> Je jette avec grâce mon feutre,[1]
> Je fais lentement l'abandon
> Du grand manteau qui me calfeutre,
> Et je tire mon espadon;
> Elégant comme Céladon,
> Agile comme Scaramouche,
> Je vous préviens, cher Mirmydon,
> Qu'à la fin de l'envoi je touche!

(*Premiers engagements de fer.*)

---

[1] My felt hat I throw down with grace,
Slowly I take off my great cloak
Which keeps me warm and comfortable,
And I draw my broadsword;
Elegant as Céladon,
Agile as Scaramouche,
I warn you, dear Mirmydon,
That at the end of the refrain, I shall thrust!

(*First collision of the swords.*)

Vous auriez bien dû rester neutre;
Où vais-je vous larder, dindon?
Dans le flanc, sous votre maheutre?
Au cœur, sous votre bleu cordon?
Les coquilles tintent, ding-don!
Ma pointe voltige: une mouche!
Décidément—c'est au bedon,
Qu'à la fin de l'envoi je touche.

Il me manque une rime en eutre—
Vous rompez, plus blanc qu'amidon?
C'est pour me fourmir le mot pleutre!
    Tac! Je pare la pointe dont
Vous espériez me faire don;
J'ouvre la ligne,—je la bouche—
Tiens bien ta broche, Laridon!
À la fin de l'envoi, je touche.

(*Il annonce solennellement:*) Envoi.

Prince, demande à Dieu pardon!
Je quarte du pied, j'escaramouche,

You would have done well to remain neutral;
Where shall I lard you, turkey?
In the side, under your sleeve?
In the heart, under your blue badge?
The sword-hilts ring, ding-dong!
My point flutters about like a fly!
Decidedly—it is in the belly
That at the end of the refrain, I shall **thrust!**

I need another rhyme—
You break off, whiter than chalk?
In order to furnish me the word **coward!**
There! I parry the point which
You hoped to give to me;—
I open the line,—I block it up,—
Hold your spit well, Laridon!
At the end of the refrain, I shall **thrust.**

(*He announces solemnly:*) Envoi.

Prince, ask God to pardon you!
I guard, I flourish my sword,

48

Cyrano de Bergerac

Je coupe, je feinte—(*se fendant*).
Hé! là donc

(*Le* Vicomte *chancelle;* CYRANO *salue.*)

À la fin de l'envoi, je touche.

(*Cheers. Applause in the boxes. A rain of flowers and hand-kerchiefs.* Officers *surround and congratulate* CYRANO. RAGUE-NEAU *dances enthusiastically.* LE BRET *is both happy and distressed. The* Viscount's *friends hold him up and conduct him away.*)

THE CROWD (*in one long shout*). Ah!

A LIGHT-HORSEMAN. Superb!

A WOMAN. Prettily done!

RAGUENEAU. Marvellous!

A MARQUIS. A novelty!

LE BRET. He is mad!

(*In the confusion around Cyrano are heard*) Compliments
—congratulations—bravo!

A WOMAN'S VOICE. He is a hero.

A MUSKETEER (*approaching Cyrano in haste, and offering his hand*). Sir, will you allow me? It was very well done, and I believe I am a judge; however, I have expressed my delight by stamping!

(*He withdraws.*)

CYRANO (*to Cuigy*). What is this gentleman's name?

CUIGY. D'Artagnan.

LE BRET (*to Cyrano, taking his arm*). Now, let us have a talk!

CYRANO. Let some of this rabble get away. (*To Bellerose.*) May I remain?

BELLEROSE (*respectfully*). Oh, certainly!

I cut, I lunge. (*Lunging.*)
Ha! There now

(*The* Viscount *staggers;* CYRANO *bows.*)

At the end of the refrain, I thrust.

(*Shouts are heard outside.*)

JODELET (*who has been looking out*). They are hooting Montfleury!

BELLEROSE (*solemnly*). *Sic transit!* (*Changing his tone: to the Doorkeeper and the candle-snuffer.*) Sweep. Close the doors, but don't put out the lights. We are coming back after dinner to rehearse a new play for to-morrow.

(JODELET *and* BELLEROSE *go out, after bowing low to* CYRANO.)

THE DOORKEEPER (*to Cyrano*). Aren't you going to dine?

CYRANO. I? No.

(*The* Doorkeeper *retires.*)

LE BRET (*to Cyrano*). Why not?

CYRANO (*proudly*). Because (*changing his tone, on seeing that the Doorkeeper has gone*)— I have no money!

LE BRET (*making the motion of throwing a bag*). What! The bag of crowns?

CYRANO. Paternal allowance, gone in a single day!

LE BRET. How will you live for a whole month, then?

CYRANO. I have nothing left.

LE BRET. How foolish to throw away that bag!

CYRANO. But how well done!

THE REFRESHMENT GIRL (*coughing behind her little counter*). Hem! (*Cyrano and Le Bret turning around, she approaches, somewhat abashed.*) Sir—to know you're fasting—breaks my heart. (*Pointing to the refreshment table.*) I have there everything necessary. (*Eagerly.*) Take what you like!

CYRANO (*removing his hat*). My dear child, although my Gascony pride forbids me to accept the least delicacy from your fingers, I am so much afraid of hurting your feelings by refusing, that I will accept— (*He goes to the stand and makes a selection.*) Oh, some little thing!—a grape— (*She wishes to give him the bunch; he picks off one grape.*) Only one!— This glass of (*she wishes to pour in some wine; he stops her*) clear water! And half a macaroon! (*He puts back the other half.*)

LE BRET. How stupid!

THE REFRESHMENT GIRL. Oh, something more!

CYRANO. Yes. Your hand to kiss.

(*He kisses the hand she offers to him as if it were the hand of a princess.*)

THE REFRESHMENT GIRL. Thank you, sir. (*She courtesies.*) Good evening. (*She goes out.*)

SCENE FIFTH

CYRANO, LE BRET, *then the* Doorkeeper

CYRANO (*to Le Bret*). I will listen to you now. (*He places himself in front of the refreshment stand and puts the macaroon before him.*) Dinner! (*Then the glass of water.*) Drink! (*The grape.*) Dessert! (*He sits down.*) Now I will sit down to table! Ah! I was terribly hungry, my dear! (*Eating.*) You were saying?

LE BRET. That these fops with their grand warlike airs will spoil your wit if you listen only to them! Go, consult people of good sense, and find out the effect of your sudden outburst of passion.

CYRANO (*finishing his macaroon*). Prodigious.

LE BRET. The Cardinal—

CYRANO. Was the Cardinal there?

LE BRET. Must have found it—

CYRANO. Very original.

LE BRET. And yet—

CYRANO. He is an author. It cannot displease him to have a brother writer's play disturbed.

LE BRET. You are really getting too many enemies on your hands!

CYRANO (*attacking his grape*). About how many have I made this evening?

LE BRET. Forty-eight. Without counting the women.

53

CYRANO. Let us see, reckon them up!

LE BRET. Montfleury, the tradesman, De Guiche, the Viscount, Baro, the Academy—

CYRANO. Enough! You delight me!

LE BRET. But where will your mode of life lead you? What is your plan?

CYRANO. I wandered in a maze; I had too many and too complicated courses to decide upon; so I took—

LE BRET. Which?

CYRANO. By far the simplest. I decided to be worthy of admiration in all things, for all!

LE BRET (*shrugging his shoulders*). So be it! But tell me the real motive of your hatred for Montfleury!

CYRANO (*rising*). That Silenus, so corpulent that he cannot reach below his belt, still believes himself dangerously attractive to the women; and rolls his great frogs' eyes at them, while he stammers through the play! And I have hated him since he allowed his glance one evening to fall upon her— Oh! I thought I saw a long slug crawling over a flower!

LE BRET (*dumfounded*). Eh? What? Can it be possible?

CYRANO (*with a bitter laugh*). That I should be in love? (*Changing his tone and speaking gravely.*) I am in love.

LE BRET. May I know? Have you never told me?

CYRANO. Whom I love? Think of it. That nose, which is a quarter of an hour ahead of me everywhere I go, forbids me to dream of being loved even by the plainest, so whom do I love? A matter of course! I love—I couldn't help it!—the loveliest of all!

LE BRET. The loveliest?

CYRANO. Simply the loveliest in the world! The most brilliant, the most clever (*despondently*), the fairest!

LE BRET. Heavens, who is this woman?

CYRANO. A mortal danger without intending to be so, exquisite without dreaming of it, a snare of nature, a musk rose where love is held in ambush! Whoever knows her smile has known perfection. She is nothing if not graceful, her slightest

54

gesture is wholly divine. And thou, O Venus, couldst never mount thy boat of shell, or thou, O Diana, stride through the mighty forests full of bloom, as she ascends her Sedan chair or glides along the Paris streets.

LE BRET. Sapristi! I understand. It is quite clear!

CYRANO. It is transparent.

LE BRET. Magdeleine Robin, your cousin?

CYRANO. Yes, Roxane.

LE BRET. Ah! well. It is the best thing that could happen! You love her? Tell her so! You have covered yourself with glory, in her eyes, to-day!

CYRANO. Look at me, my dear fellow, and tell me what hope this protuberance could possibly leave me! Oh! I don't allow myself any illusions!—Heavens, yes, sometimes I grow sentimental at violet evening; I go into some garden where the hour is full of perfume; with my poor devil of a nose I breathe in the April air,—with my eyes I follow, in the silvery light, some woman on her lover's arm, and I fancy that I, too, should like to walk slowly in the moonlight with some one on my arm. I am exalted. I forget—and suddenly I notice the shadow of my profile on the garden wall!

LE BRET (*touched*). My friend!

CYRANO. My friend, I have unhappy hours when I feel that I am so ugly, and sometimes all alone—

LE BRET (*quickly taking his hand*). You weep?

CYRANO. Ah! no, never that! No, it would be too ugly if a tear should roll along this nose! I would never allow the divine beauty of tears, as long as I am master of them, to be exposed to such gross ugliness! There is nothing more sublime, you see, than tears, nothing, and I would not have one made ridiculous by exciting laughter!

LE BRET. Come, don't be melancholy! Love is but chance!

CYRANO (*shaking his head*). No! I love Cleopatra: do I look like Cæsar? I adore Berenice: do I appear like a Titus?

LE BRET. But your courage! Your wit! The little girl who

55

offered you, just now, that modest repast,—you saw plainly that her eyes did not find you detestable!

CYRANO (*impressed*). That is true!

LE BRET. Ah! Well, then? Roxane herself turned pale as she watched your duel!

CYRANO. Turned pale?

LE BRET. Her heart and her mind are already moved to wonder! Venture to speak to her in order that—

CYRANO. That she may laugh at my nose? No! That is the only thing in the world I fear.

THE DOORKEEPER (*bringing some one in to Cyrano*). Sir, some one is asking for you—

CYRANO (*seeing the Duenna*). Ah, Heavens, her duenna!

SCENE SIXTH

CYRANO, LE BRET, *the* Duenna

THE DUENNA (*bowing low*). Some one is anxious to know where her brave cousin can be seen secretly.

CYRANO (*agitated*). See me?

THE DUENNA (*courtesying*). See you. There is something to be said to you.

CYRANO. Something?

THE DUENNA (*courtesying again*). Something!

CYRANO (*staggering*). Oh, my God!

THE DUENNA. She will go to-morrow at the earliest dawn—to hear mass at Saint Roch.

CYRANO (*supporting himself against Le Bret*). Oh! my God!

THE DUENNA. On the way out, where could one go to have a little talk?

CYRANO (*carried away*). Where?—I—but—Oh! my God!

THE DUENNA. Tell me quickly.

CYRANO. I am trying to think.

THE DUENNA. Where?

CYRANO. At—at—Ragueneau's—the pastry-cook's.

THE DUENNA. Where is he?

CYRANO. In Rue—Oh! my God! my God!—Saint Honoré—

THE DUENNA (*going away*). She will go. Be there at seven o'clock.

CYRANO. I will be there.

(*The Duenna goes out.*)

SCENE SEVENTH

CYRANO, LE BRET, *then the* Actors *and* Actresses, CUIGY, BRIS-SAILLE, LIGNIÈRE, *the* Doorkeeper, *the* Violinists.

CYRANO (*falling into Le Bret's arms*). To me!—from her!— A rendezvous!

LE BRET. Well, now you are no longer sad?

CYRANO. Ah! whatever it may be, she is aware of my existence!

LE BRET. Now you will be calm?

CYRANO (*beside himself*). Now—I shall be frantic and furious! I must have a whole army to put to flight! I have ten hearts; I have twenty arms; I am not content with slaying dwarfs. I must have giants! (*He shouts at the top of his voice.*) I must have giants!

(*For a moment at the back of the stage shadows of* Actors *and* Actresses *have been moving about, whispering; they begin to rehearse. The* Violins *have taken their places.*)

A VOICE (*from the stage.*) Sh! Pst! Silence down there! We are rehearsing here!

CYRANO (*laughing*). We are going!

(*He goes toward the back; through the large door at the back enter* CUIGY, BRISSAILLE, *several* Officers *supporting* LIGNIÈRE, *who is completely intoxicated.*)

57

CUIGY. Cyrano!

CYRANO. What is it?

CUIGY. A huge thrush that we are bringing to you!

CYRANO (*recognizing him*). Lignière! Hallo! what has happened to you?

CUIGY. He is looking for you!

BRISSAILLE. He can't go home!

CYRANO. Why?

LIGNIÈRE (*in a thick voice, showing him a very crumpled note*). This note warns me—a hundred men against me—on account of—song—great danger threatens me—Porte de Nesle —I have to pass through it to get back—allow me to sleep at your—at your house!

CYRANO. A hundred men, did you say? You shall sleep at your own house!

LIGNIÈRE (*dismayed*). But—

CYRANO (*in a terrible voice, pointing to the lighted lantern which the Doorkeeper is swinging as he listens curiously to what is said*). Take that lantern!

LIGNIÈRE (*hurriedly seizes the lantern*).

CYRANO. And walk along! I swear to you that I will see that you are safely tucked in bed! (*To the Officers.*) You! Follow at a distance, and be witnesses!

CUIGY. But a hundred men!

CYRANO. To-night I need no less!

(*The Actors and the Actresses having come down from the stage draw near in their various costumes.*)

LE BRET. But why protect—

CYRANO. There is Le Bret grumbling!

LE BRET. That vulgar drunkard?

CYRANO (*slapping Lignière on the shoulder*). Because this drunkard, this barrel of muscatel, this cask of rossoli, one day did a very pretty thing: coming out from mass he saw his sweetheart take some holy water according to the custom, and he who runs away from water hastened to the basin, bent over it, and drank it every drop!

AN ACTRESS (*in soubrette costume*). Ah, that was sweet, it was!

CYRANO. Wasn't it?

THE ACTRESS (*to the others*). But why are there a hundred against one poor poet?

CYRANO. Let us away! (*To the Officers.*) And you, sirs, when you see me charge do not second me, no matter what the danger may be!

ANOTHER ACTRESS (*rushing from the stage*). Oh! but I am going to see!

CYRANO. Come along!

ANOTHER (*rushing toward an old Actor*). Are you coming, Cassandra?

CYRANO. Come all of you, the doctor, Isabelle, Léandre, all of you! For you are going to join a charming, giddy throng, the Italian farce to this Spanish drama, and above its roar ringing a fantastic din, surround it with bells like a tambourine!

ALL THE WOMEN (*dancing for joy*). Bravo!—Quick, a cloak! A hood!

JODELET. Let us go!

CYRANO (*to the Violins*). You shall play a tune, violins!

(*The* Violins *join in the procession forming. They seize the lighted candles from the footlights and distribute them. It becomes a torchlight procession.*)

Bravo! Officers, women in costume, and twenty steps forward, (*He takes his place as he speaks.*) Myself, all alone, under the plume which Glory herself raised in this hat, thrice as proud as a Scipio. Nasica!—Is it understood? You are forbidden to lend me assistance! All ready?—One, two, three! Doorkeeper, open the door! (*The Doorkeeper opens the double doors. A corner of picturesque old Paris by moonlight is seen.*) Ah!— Paris melts away, by night, and grows mistlike; the moonlight flows over the slopes of her bluish roofs; an exquisite framework is prepared for this scene; below, under the scarf of vapors, the Seine like a mysterious, magic mirror, trembles.— And you will see what you will see!

ALL. To the Porte de Nesle!

CYRANO (*standing on the threshold*). To the Porte de Nesle! (*Before he goes, turns to the Soubrette.*) Didn't you ask, mademoiselle, why a hundred men were sent against this lone rhymester? (*He draws his sword and adds, calmly*) It is because they knew that he is one of my friends!

(*He goes out. The procession with* LIGNIÈRE *staggering along at the head,—then the* Actresses *on the* Officers' *arms,—then the* Actors, *frisking, march into the darkness to the sound of the violins, and the flickering light of the candles.*)
Curtain falls.

ACT SECOND

The Poet's Cook Shop

The shop of RAGUENEAU, *meat and pastry-cook, a large bakery on the corner of Rue Saint Honoré and Rue de l'Arbre-Sec. A broad view of the streets gray in the first light of the dawn is seen at the back through the glass windows of the door.*

On the left, foreground, a counter with a wrought-iron canopy, to which are fastened geese, ducks, and white peacocks. In large china vases, tall bouquets of natural flowers, principally yellow sunflowers. On the same side, farther back, an immense fireplace in front of which, between monstrous andirons, each supporting a small pot, roasts are dripping into pans.

On the right, foreground, a door. Farther back, a staircase leading to a little room in a loft, the interior of which is seen through open shutters; in it a table is laid, a slender Flemish chandelier lights it: it is a nook where people can have refreshments. A wooden gallery, a continuation of the staircase, appears to lead to other similar small rooms.

In the middle of the cook shop, an iron ring which can be let down by means of a cord, and to which large pieces of game are fastened, makes a sort of chandelier.

The ovens glow in the shadow under the staircase. The copper vessels shine. Spits are turning. Mounted pieces of game form a pyramid. Hams are hung up here and there. It is the bustle of early morning. Confusion of bewildered scullions, huge cooks, and small apprentices. Caps abundantly trimmed with hen's feathers or guinea-fowl's wings. Quincunxes of brioches, villages of pastry, are brought in on sheet-iron plates and osier stands.

61

Some tables are covered with cakes and dishes. Others, surrounded by chairs, are ready for those wishing to eat and drink. One smaller than the others, in a corner, is lost under papers. RAGUENEAU *is seated at it writing, when the curtain rises.*

SCENE FIRST

RAGUENEAU, Pastry-cooks, *then* LISE; RAGUENEAU, *at the small table, writing with an inspired air, and counting on his fingers.*

FIRST PASTRY-COOK (*bringing a fancy confection*). Fruits in nougat!

SECOND PASTRY-COOK (*bringing a dish*). Custard!

THIRD PASTRY-COOK (*bringing a roast decorated with feathers*). Peacock!

FOURTH PASTRY-COOK (*bringing a plate of cakes*). Roinsoles!

FIFTH PASTRY-COOK (*bringing a sort of pan*). Beef stew!

RAGUENEAU (*stops writing, and raising his head*). The dawn's silver light is already stealing over the brasses! Stifle within thee the god of song, Ragueneau! The time for the lute will come,—it is now time for the oven! (*He rises. To a Cook.*) Will you lengthen out this sauce, it is short!

THE COOK. How much?

RAGUENEAU. Three feet!

(*He passes along.*)

THE COOK. What?

FIRST PASTRY-COOK. The tart!

SECOND PASTRY-COOK. The pie!

RAGUENEAU (*in front of the fireplace*). Leave me, O Muse, that your charming eyes may not be reddened by the fire of these vine-branches! (*To a Pastry-cook, showing him some bread.*) You have not slit these loaves in the right place: the cæsura,—between the hemistiches! (*To another, showing him an unfinished pastry.*) You must put a roof on this palace of crust. (*To a young Apprentice, who is seated on the floor, putting poultry on a spit.*) And you, my son, upon that interminable spit alternate the modest chicken and the haughty turkey, as old Malherbe alternated long lines with very short ones, and turn to the fire your strophied roasts!

ANOTHER APPRENTICE (*approaching with a tray covered with a napkin*). Master, I thought of you and had this baked, which I hope will please you.

(*He uncovers the tray, and shows a large lyre of pastry.*)

RAGUENEAU (*dazzled*). A lyre!

THE APPRENTICE. Of puff paste.

RAGUENEAU (*touched*). With preserved fruit!

THE APPRENTICE. And the strings, you see, I have made of sugar.

RAGUENEAU (*giving him some money*). Go, drink my health! (*Seeing Lise come in.*) Hush! my wife! Be off, and hide that money! (*To Lise, showing her the lyre, and looking uneasy.*) Isn't that fine?

LISE. It is ridiculous!

(*She places a pile of paper bags on the counter.*)

RAGUENEAU. Bags? Good. Thank you. (*He looks at them.*) Heavens! My revered books! The verses of my friends! Torn! Pulled apart! To make bags to put pies in. Oh, you repeat Orpheus and the bacchants!

LISE (*dryly*). And really haven't I the right to utilize what your wretched writers of uneven lines leave here as their only pay!

RAGUENEAU. Pismire! Do not insult these divine cicadæ!

LISE. Before you associated with those people, you never called me a bacchant,—nor an ant!

RAGUENEAU. To do such a thing as that with verses!

LISE. There was nothing else to do.

RAGUENEAU. What did you do, then, with the prose, madame?

SCENE SECOND

The Same. Two Children, *who have just come into the bakery*

RAGUENEAU. What would you like, children?

FIRST CHILD. Three patties.

RAGUENEAU (*serving them*). There, very brown—and hot.

SECOND CHILD. Will you please wrap them up?

RAGUENEAU (*disturbed, aside*). Alas! One of my bags! (*To the Children.*) You want them wrapped up? (*He takes a bag, and, just as he is going to put in the patties, reads:*) "So Ulysses, the day he left Penelope—" Not that one! (*He puts it aside and takes another. Just as he is putting the patties in this, he reads:*) "Fair Phœbus—" Not that!

(*Puts that aside also.*)

LISE (*impatiently*). Well! What are you waiting for?

RAGUENEAU. There, there, there! (*He takes a third, and is resigned.*) The sonnet to Phyllis!—but it is hard, all the same!

LISE. Fortunately he has decided! (*Shrugging her shoulders.*) Nicodemus!

(*She climbs into a chair, and begins to arrange the dishes in a cupboard.*)

RAGUENEAU (*profiting by the fact that her back is turned, calls back the Children, who are already at the door*). Pst—children! Give me back the sonnet to Phyllis, and I will give you six patties instead of three. (*The Children give him back the bag, seize the cakes quickly, and go out. Ragueneau, smoothing out the paper, begins to read, declaiming:*) "Phyllis!" A butter stain on this sweet name!—"Phyllis!"

(*Enter* CYRANO *hurriedly.*)

SCENE THIRD

RAGUENEAU, LISE, CYRANO, *then the* Musketeer

CYRANO. What time is it?

RAGUENEAU (*bowing to him cordially*). Six o'clock.

CYRANO (*with emotion*). In an hour!

(*He walks back and forth in the shop.*)

RAGUENEAU (*following him*). Bravo! I saw—

CYRANO. What do you mean?

RAGUENEAU. Your combat!

CYRANO. Which one?

RAGUENEAU. The one at the Hôtel de Bourgogne!

CYRANO (*disdainfully*). Oh! the duel!

RAGUENEAU. (*admiringly*). Yes, the duel in verse!

LISE. He knows it by heart!

CYRANO. Good for him!

RAGUENEAU (*lunging with a spit he has seized*). How fine that is! (*With increasing enthusiasm.*)

CYRANO. What time is it, Ragueneau?

RAGUENEAU (*stopping to look at the clock*). Five minutes past six! (*He rises.*) Oh! to compose a ballad!

LISE (*to Cyrano, who has pressed her hand absent-mindedly as he passed in front of her counter*). What is the matter with your hand?

CYRANO. Nothing; only a cut.

RAGUENEAU. Have you been in some danger?

CYRANO. No danger.

LISE (*shaking her finger at him*). I believe you are telling me a lie!

CYRANO. Did my nose move? It would take an enormous lie for that! (*Changing his tone.*) I am waiting here for some one. If I do not wait in vain you will leave us alone.

RAGUENEAU. I cannot do so; my rhymers are coming.

LISE (*ironically*). For their breakfast.

CYRANO. You must send them away when I give you a sign. What time is it?

RAGUENEAU. Ten minutes past six.

CYRANO (*seating himself nervously at Ragueneau's table and taking some paper*). A pen?

RAGUENEAU (*offering him the one he had behind his ear*). A swan's quill.

A MUSKETEER (*with splendid mustache, enters and in a stentorian voice*) Hail!

(LISE *goes quickly toward him.*)

CYRANO (*turning around*). Who is it?

RAGUENEAU. A friend of my wife's. A terrible warrior—according to his own account!

CYRANO (*taking up the pen again, and motioning Ragueneau away*). Hush! Write—fold it—(*To himself.*) Give it to her,—hurry away. (*Throwing down the pen.*) Coward! Let me die if I dare speak to her, tell her a single word— (*To Ragueneau.*) What is the time?

RAGUENEAU. Quarter past six!

CYRANO (*beating his breast*). One single word of all that I have here! While writing— (*He takes up his pen again.*) Ah! well! Let us write this love letter that I have written over and over again a hundred times in my mind, so that it is ready, and putting my soul beside the paper, I have simply to copy it.

(*He writes. Slender, hesitating shadows seen moving behind the glass window in the door.*)

SCENE FOURTH

RAGUENEAU, LISE, *the* Musketeer, CYRANO (*writing at the small table. The Poets, dressed in black, their stockings down, covered with mud*).

LISE (*entering, to Ragueneau*). Here they are, your dirty fellows!

FIRST POET (*entering, to Ragueneau*). Colleague!

SECOND POET (*the same, shaking his hands*). Dear colleague!

THIRD POET. Eagle of pastry-cooks! (*He sniffs the air.*) It smells good in your eyry.

FOURTH POET. O Phœbus, baker!

FIFTH POET. Apollo, master-cook!

RAGUENEAU (*as they surround him, embrace him, and shake hands with him*). How quickly one feels at ease with them!

FIRST POET. We were delayed by the crowd gathered at the Porte de Nesle!

SECOND POET. Eight bloody vagabonds, ripped open by the sword, illustrated the pavement!

CYRANO (*raising his head for a moment*). Eight? Wait, I thought seven.

(*He goes on with his letter.*)

RAGUENEAU (*to Cyrano*). Do you know the hero of the combat?

CYRANO (*carelessly*). I? No!

LISE (*to the Musketeer*). And you?

THE MUSKETEER (*twisting his mustache*). Perhaps.

CYRANO (*writing, aside; he is heard murmuring a word from time to time*). I love you—

FIRST POET. A single man, they assured me, was able to put a whole troop to flight!

SECOND POET. Oh, it was a strange sight! The ground was strewn with pikes and sticks!

CYRANO (*writing*). Your eyes—

THIRD POET. Hats were found as far as the *quai des Orfévres!*

FIRST POET. Sapristi! It must have been a fierce—

CYRANO (*the same action*). Your lips—

FIRST POET. A terrible giant is the author of these exploits!

CYRANO (*the same action*). And I faint with fear when my eyes rest upon you.

SECOND POET (*snatching a cake*). What new rhymes have you made, Ragueneau?

CYRANO (*the same action*). Who loves you. (*He stops just as he is about to sign his name, and rises, putting the letter in his doublet.*) No need to sign it. I will give it to her myself.

RAGUENEAU (*to the Second Poet*). I have put a receipt into verse.

THIRD POET (*placing himself near a tray of cream puffs*). Let us hear these verses!

FOURTH POET (*looking at a brioche which he has taken*). This *brioche* has put its cap on crooked.

(*He takes off the top at one bite.*)

FIRST POET. This gingerbread follows the starving rhymer with its almond eyes beneath angelic brows.

(*He takes the piece of gingerbread.*)

SECOND POET. We are listening.

THIRD POET (*pressing a puff lightly between his fingers*). This puff drools its cream. It is laughing.

SECOND POET (*biting the big pastry lyre*). For the first time, the lyre feeds me!

RAGUENEAU (*who is ready to recite, and has coughed, settled his cap, and taken his position*). A receipt in verse.

SECOND POET (*to the First, nudging him*). Are you breakfasting?

FIRST POET (*to the Second*). Are you dining?

RAGUENEAU. How to make almond tartlets:

> Battez pour qu'ils soient mousseux [1]
>   Quelques œufs;
> Incorporez à leur mousse
> Un jus de cédrat choisi;
>   Versez-y
> Un bon lait d'amande douce.

---

[1] Beat till they be foamy
  Several eggs;
Incorporate in their froth
A little choice cedrat juice;
  Then pour in
Good fresh almond milk.

Mettez de la pâte à flan
    Dans le flanc
De moules à tartelette;
D'un doigt preste, abricotez
    Les cotés;
Versez goutte à gouttelette

Votre mousse en ces puits, puis
    Que ces puits
Passent au four, et blondines,
Sortant en gais troupelets
    Ce sont les
Tartelettes amandines.

THE POETS (*with their mouths full*). Exquisite! Delicious!
A POET (*choking*). Humph!
(*They go to the back of the stage, eating.* CYRANO, *who has been watching them, goes toward* RAGUENEAU.)
CYRANO. Lulled by your voice, do you not see how they are stuffing themselves?
RAGUENEAU (*lower, with a smile*). I see it, without looking for fear of disturbing them. To repeat my verses thus gives me a double pleasure, since I satisfy a gentle weakness of mine for letting those who are hungry have something to eat!
CYRANO (*slapping him on the shoulder*). Oh, you please me! (*Ragueneau goes to rejoin his friends. Cyrano follows him with his eyes, then somewhat abruptly.*) Ho there, Lise? (*Lise, in tender conversation with the Musketeer, trembles, and goes toward Cyrano.*) Does the captain—besiege you?

Put the custard
    In the moulds.
With a deft finger close
    The sides;
Then pour drop by drop

Your foamy custard into these pits,
    Then let these pits
Go to the oven, and when
They come forth light brown
They will be gay troupes
Of almond tartlets.

LISE (*offended*). Oh! my eyes with a haughty glance know how to conquer any one who dares to attack my virtues.

CYRANO. Ugh! Your eyes for conquerors to me look very much beaten.

LISE (*choking*). But—

CYRANO (*decidedly*). I like Ragueneau; that is why, Dame Lise, I forbid any one to make him ridiculous.

LISE. But—

CYRANO (*who has raised his voice enough to be heard by the gallant*). A word to the wise—

(*He bows to the* Musketeer, *and, after looking at the clock, takes up a place of observation by the door at the back.*)

LISE (*to the Musketeer, who has merely returned Cyrano's bow*). Really, you astonish me! Reply—on his nose—

THE MUSKETEER. On his nose—on his nose—

(*He moves away quickly;* LISE *follows.*)

CYRANO (*from the door at the back signing to Ragueneau to take away the Poets*). Pst!

RAGUENEAU (*showing the door on the right to the Poets*). We shall be much better in there—

CYRANO (*impatiently*). Pst! Pst!

RAGUENEAU (*pulling them along*). To read the verses—

FIRST POET (*in despair, with his mouth full*). But the cakes!

SECOND POET. Bring them along!

(*They all go out behind* RAGUENEAU, *in a procession, and after making a clean sweep of the trays.*)

SCENE FIFTH

CYRANO, ROXANE, *the* Duenna

CYRANO. I will take out my letter if I feel there is the least hope! (*Roxane, masked, followed by the Duenna, appears be-*

hind the window. He quickly opens the door.) Come in! (*Stepping up to the Duenna.*) Two words with you, Duenna!

THE DUENNA. Four.

CYRANO. Are you fond of cakes?

THE DUENNA. Fond enough to make myself sick with them.

CYRANO (*quickly taking up some paper bags on the counter*). Good! Here are two sonnets by Monsieur Benserade—

THE DUENNA. Alas!

CYRANO. Which I will fill for you with cream cakes.

THE DUENNA (*changing her face*). Oh!

CYRANO. Do you like the cakes called puffs?

THE DUENNA. I am very fond of them when there is cream in them.

CYRANO. I will plunge six of them for you into the bosom of a poem by Saint-Amant! And in these verses by Chapelain I will put a piece of sponge cake of lighter weight.—Ah! you like fresh cakes?

THE DUENNA. I'm in love with them!

CYRANO (*loading her arms with well-filled bags*). Please go and eat all these in the street.

THE DUENNA. But—

CYRANO (*pushing her out*). And don't come back until you have finished them!

(*He closes the door, goes back to* ROXANE, *and taking off his hat, stops at a respectful distance.*)

SCENE SIXTH

CYRANO, ROXANE, *the* Duenna, *for a moment*

CYRANO. May this moment above all other moments be blessed, when, ceasing to forget that I humbly exist, you come here to tell me—to tell me?

ROXANE (*after unmasking*). But first of all let me thank you because that knave, that fop, you check-mated in brave sword-play, yesterday is the one, a great lord—in love with me—

CYRANO. De Guiche?

ROXANE (*dropping her eyes*). Tried to impose upon me—for a husband.

CYRANO. A substitute? (*Bowing.*) Then I have fought, and so much the better, not for my ugly nose, but for your lovely eyes.

ROXANE. Then—I wished— But for the confession I am going to make, I must think of you once more as the—almost brother—I used to play with in the park—near the lake!

CYRANO. Yes—you used to come every summer to Bergerac!

ROXANE. The reeds furnished the wood for your swords—

CYRANO. And the maize, the light hair for your dolls!

ROXANE. It was the time for games—

CYRANO. And wild berries—

ROXANE. The time when you did everything I wished!

CYRANO. Roxane, in short dresses, called Magdeleine—

ROXANE. Was I pretty, then?

CYRANO. You were not ugly.

ROXANE. Sometimes you came running with your hand all bleeding from climbing! Then playing mamma, I would say, trying to make my voice severe: (*She takes his hand.*) "What is the meaning of this scratch?" (*She stops in surprise.*) Oh! This is too bad! It really is! (*Cyrano tries to draw away his hand.*) No! Show it to me! What? At your age, still? Where did you do that?

CYRANO. While playing, near the Porte de Nesle.

ROXANE (*sitting down at a table, and dipping her handkerchief in a glass of water*). Give it to me!

CYRANO (*also sitting down*). So prettily! So blithely maternal!

ROXANE. Tell me—while I wipe away a little of the blood—there were against you?

CYRANO. Oh, not quite a hundred.

ROXANE. Tell me about it!

CYRANO. No. Let it pass. But tell me what it is that you were afraid to speak of just now—

ROXANE (*still holding his hand*). Now I am not afraid, for the perfume of the past encourages me! Yes, now, I dare to tell you. There. I am in love with some one.

CYRANO. Ah!

ROXANE. Who does not know it, however.

CYRANO. Ah!

ROXANE. Not yet.

CYRANO. Ah!

ROXANE. But who will know it soon, if he is not aware of it now.

CYRANO. Ah!

ROXANE. A poor fellow who until now has loved me timidly, afar off, without daring to speak of it.

CYRANO. Ah!

ROXANE. Give me your hand; see, it is feverish.—But I saw his confession trembling on his lips.

CYRANO. Ah!

ROXANE (*finishes making him a little bandage with her handkerchief*). And just imagine it, it is really so, my cousin; he serves in your regiment!

CYRANO. Ah!

ROXANE (*laughing*). For he is a cadet in your company!

CYRANO. Ah!

ROXANE. His face glows with wit, with genius; he is proud, noble, young, fearless, handsome—

CYRANO (*rising, very pale*). Handsome!

ROXANE. What is it? What is the matter?

CYRANO. With me? Nothing— It is— It is— (*He shows her his hand with a smile.*) It is this trifling hurt.

ROXANE. In short, I love him. Moreover, I must tell you that I have never seen him except at the play.

CYRANO. You have never yet spoken to each other?

ROXANE. With our eyes alone.

CYRANO. But how do you know, then?

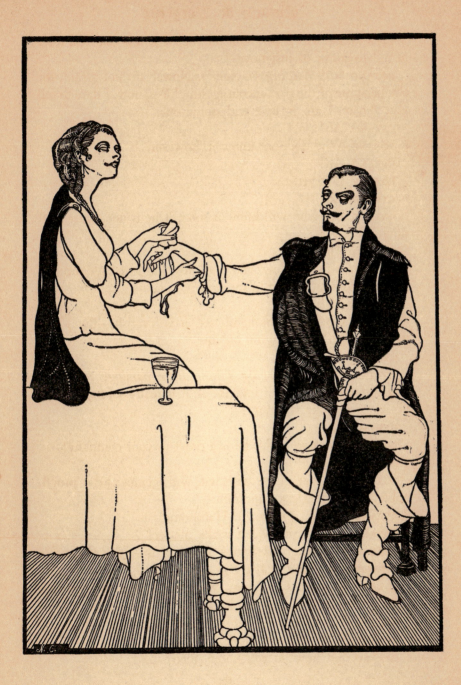

ROXANE. Under the lindens in the Place Royale people talk. Gossips have told me.

CYRANO. He is a cadet?

ROXANE. He is, in the guards.

CYRANO. His name?

ROXANE. Baron Christian de Neuvillette.

CYRANO. What? He is not in the cadets.

ROXANE. Yes, since this morning: Captain Carbon de Castel-Jaloux.

CYRANO. How quickly one can throw away one's heart. But, my poor little girl—

THE DUENNA (*opening the door at the back of the stage*). I have finished the cakes, Monsieur de Bergerac!

CYRANO. Well! Read the verses printed on the bag! (*The Duenna disappears.*) My poor child, you who love only fine speech, wit—if he should be unlearned, uncultivated.

ROXANE. No, he has the hair of one of D'Urfé's heroes!

CYRANO. If his speech should be as awkward as his hair is beautiful!

ROXANE. No, every word he says is clever, I am sure!

CYRANO. Yes, all words are fine when the face is fine. But if he is stupid!

ROXANE (*stamping her foot*). Well! Then I should die!

CYRANO (*after a time*). Have you brought me here to tell me that? I do not see much use in it, madame.

ROXANE. Ah, it was because yesterday some one broke my heart by telling me that all of you, every one, in your company, are Gascons—

CYRANO. And that we challenge all the simpletons who, through favor, get admitted among the pure Gascons, such as we are, without being so themselves? Is that what they told you?

ROXANE. You can imagine how I trembled for him.

CYRANO (*between his teeth*). Not without reason.

ROXANE. But I thought when invincible and great you appeared to us yesterday, chastising that rascal, coping with those brutes,—I thought, if he would, he whom they all fear—

CYRANO. Very good, I will defend your little baron.

ROXANE. Oh, you will defend him for me, will you not? I have always felt such a tender friendship for you.

CYRANO. Yes, yes.

ROXANE. You will be his friend?

CYRANO. I will.

ROXANE. And he shall never have a duel?

CYRANO. I swear it.

ROXANE. Oh! I love you dearly. I must go. (*She quickly replaces her mask and the lace over her forehead, and absentmindedly:*) But you haven't told me about the battle that night. Really it must have been unheard of!—Tell him to write to me. (*She throws him a little kiss.*) Oh! I love you!

CYRANO. Yes, yes.

ROXANE. A hundred men against you? Well, farewell. We are great friends!

CYRANO. Yes, yes.

ROXANE. Let him write to me!—A hundred men!—You shall tell me about it later on. Now, I cannot stay. A hundred men! What courage!

CYRANO (*bowing*). Oh! I have done better since.

(*She goes out.* CYRANO *remains motionless, his eyes on the ground. Silence. The door at the right opens.* RAGUENEAU *puts in his head.*)

SCENE SEVENTH

CYRANO, RAGUENEAU, *the* POETS, CARBON DE CASTEL-JALOUX, *the* Cadets, *a* Crowd, *etc., then* DE GUICHE.

RAGUENEAU. May we come in?

CYRANO (*without stirring*). Yes.

(RAGUENEAU *makes a sign, and his friends come in again.*

At the same time, at the door at the back appears CARBON DE CASTEL-JALOUX *in costume of captain of the guard, making extravagant gestures when he sees* CYRANO.)

CARBON DE CASTEL-JALOUX. There he is!

CYRANO (*raising his head*). My captain!

CARBON (*exulting*). Our hero! We know all! Thirty of my cadets are there.

CYRANO (*drawing back*). But—

CARBON (*anxious to take him away*). Come! They want to see you!

CYRANO. No!

CARBON. They are drinking opposite at the Croix du Trahoir.

CYRANO. I—

CARBON (*going back to the door and calling behind the scenes, in a thundering voice*). The hero refuses. He is in a crusty mood.

A VOICE (*outside*). Zounds!

(*Tumult outside, noise of swords and boots approaching.*)

CARBON (*rubbing his hands*). Here they come across the street!

(*The* Cadets *enter the cook shop, with a chorus of Gascon oaths.*)

RAGUENEAU (*drawing back in dismay*). Gentlemen, are you all from Gascony?

THE CADETS. All!

A CADET (*to Cyrano*). Bravo!

CYRANO. Baron!

ANOTHER (*shaking his hands*). Vivat!

CYRANO. Baron!

THIRD CADET. Let me embrace you!

CYRANO. Baron!

SEVERAL GASCONS. Let us embrace him!

CYRANO (*not knowing what to reply*). Baron—baron—pray—

RAGUENEAU. Are you all barons, gentlemen?

THE CADETS. All!

RAGUENEAU. Are they?

FIRST CADET. A tower could be made out of our baron's lambrequins.

LE BRET (*entering, and running to Cyrano*). They are looking for you! A frenzied crowd led by those who marched after you that night!

CYRANO (*in dismay*). You did not tell them where I was to be found!

LE BRET (*rubbing his hands*). Yes!

A TRADESMAN (*entering, followed by a number of others*). Sir, the entire Marais is coming here!

(*Outside, the street is filled with people. Sedan chairs and coaches stop.*)

LE BRET (*in a low voice, smiling, to Cyrano*). And Roxane?

CYRANO (*quickly*). Be quiet!

THE CROWD (*shouting outside*). Cyrano!

(*A tumultuous throng rushes into the cook shop. Confusion. Cheering.*)

RAGUENEAU (*standing on a table*). My shop is invaded! They are breaking everything! It is magnificent!

PEOPLE (*around Cyrano*). My friend—my friend.

CYRANO. I did not have so many friends yesterday!

LE BRET (*delighted*). What a success!

A LITTLE MARQUIS (*running with outstretched hands*). If thou knewest, my dear!

CYRANO. If thou?—Thou? What have we had together?

ANOTHER. I wish to present you, sir, to some ladies there in my carriage.

CYRANO (*coldly*). And who will first present you to me?

LE BRET (*dumfounded*). What is the matter with you?

CYRANO. Be silent!

A MAN OF LETTERS (*with an inkstand*). May I have the details about—?

CYRANO. No.

LE BRET (*nudging him with his elbow*). It is Théophraste Renaudot! the inventor of the *Gazette*.

CYRANO. Pooh!

LE BRET. That leaf made to contain so many things! They say this idea has a great future!

A POET (*advancing*). Sir—

CYRANO. Again!

THE POET. I wish to make a pentacrostic on your name—

SOME ONE ELSE (*advancing*). Sir—

CYRANO. Enough!

(*The* Crowd *moves. The people step aside.* DE GUICHE *appears escorted by officers,* CUIGY, BRISSAILLE, *and the* Officers *who went out with* CYRANO *at the end of the first act.* CUIGY *comes quickly to* CYRANO.)

CUIGY (*to Cyrano*). Monsieur de Guiche! (*Murmurs. Everybody steps aside.*) Comes in behalf of Marshal de Gassion!

DE GUICHE (*bowing to Cyrano*). Who desires to express to you his admiration for the new exploit, the report of which has just become current.

THE CROWD. Bravo!

CYRANO (*bowing*). The marshal well knows what bravery is.

DE GUICHE. He would never have believed the fact if these gentlemen could not have sworn that they had seen it.

CUIGY. With our eyes!

LE BRET (*in a low voice to Cyrano, who seems absent-minded*). But—

CYRANO. Be still!

LE BRET. You seem to be suffering!

CYRANO (*starting and quickly straightening up*). Before these people? (*His mustache bristles; he throws out his chest.*) I suffer? You shall see!

DE GUICHE (*in whose ear Cuigy has been whispering*). Your career already abounds in fine exploits. You serve among these mad Gascons, do you not?

CYRANO. In the cadets, yes.

A CADET (*in a terrible voice*). With us!

DE GUICHE (*looking at the Gascons ranged behind Cyrano*). Ah! Ah! So all these gentlemen with such haughty bearing are the famous ones?

CARBON DE CASTEL-JALOUX. Cyrano!

CYRANO. Captain?

CARBON. Since my company is, I believe, complete, will you please present them to the count.

CYRANO (*taking two steps toward De Guiche, and pointing to the Cadets*).

> Ce sont les cadets de Gascogne [1]
> De Carbon de Castel-Jaloux;
> Bretteurs et menteurs sans vergogne,
> Ce sont les cadets de Gascogne!
> Parlant blason, lambel, bastogne,
> Tous plus nobles que des filous,
> Ce sont les cadets de Gascogne
> De Carbon de Castel-Jaloux:
>
> Œil d'aigle, jambe de cigogne,
> Moustache de chat, dents de loups,
> Fendant la canaille qui grogne,
> Œil d'aigle, jambe de cigogne.
> Ils vont,—coiffés d'un vieux vigogne
> Dont la plume cache les trous!
> Œil d'aigle, jambe de cigogne,
> Moustache de chat, dents de loups!

---

[1] These are the Gascony cadets
   Of Carbon de Castel-Jaloux;
   Fighters and liars without shame,
   These are the Gascony cadets!
   Talking of heraldry, quarterings and arms,
   All far nobler than thieves,
   These are the Gascony cadets
   Of Carbon de Castel-Jaloux.

   Eagle eye, stork's leg,
   Cat's whiskers, wolf's teeth,
   Forcing their way through the grumbling crowd,
   Eagle eye, stork's leg,
   They go—wearing an old felt hat,
   The plume concealing the holes!
   Eagle eye, stork's leg,
   Cat's whiskers, wolf's teeth!

Perce-Bedaine et Casse-Trogne
Sont leurs sobriquets les plus doux;
De Gloire, leur âme est ivrogne!
Perce-Bedaine et Casse-Trogne,
Dans tous les endroits où l'on cogne
Ils se donnent des rendez-vous—
Perce-Bedaine et Casse-Trogne
Sont leurs sobriquets les plus doux!

Voici les cadets de Gascogne
Qui font cocus tous les jaloux!
O femme adorable carogne,
Voici les cadets de Gascogne!
Que le vieil époux se renfrogne:
Sonnez, clairons! chantez, coucous!
Voici les cadets de Gascogne
Qui font cocus tous les jaloux!

DE GUICHE (*seating himself carelessly in an armchair which Ragueneau has hastened to bring*). A poet is a luxury which we indulge in to-day. Will you belong to me?

CYRANO. No, sir, to no one.

Belly-Thrust and Smash-Pate
Are their favorite nicknames;
Their soul is drunk with glory!
Belly-Thrust and Smash-Pate,
Wherever there is quarrelling
There is sure to be their meeting-place.
Belly-Thrust and Smash-Pate
Are their favorite nicknames!

These are the Gascony cadets
Giving jealous husbands cause!
O woman, adorable jade,
These are the Gascony cadets!
Let the old husband frown:
Sound, trumpets! Sing, cuckoos!
These are the Gascony cadets
Giving jealous husbands cause!

DE GUICHE. Your spirit amused my uncle Richelieu yesterday. I would like to help you with him.

LE BRET (*dazzled*). Good Lord!

DE GUICHE. I believe you have written five acts in rhyme?

LE BRET (*in Cyrano's ear*). You are going to have your "Agrippine" played!

DE GUICHE. Carry them to him.

CYRANO (*tempted and rather pleased*). Really—

DE GUICHE. He is one of the most expert. He will correct some of your verses—

CYRANO (*whose face immediately grows dark*). Impossible, sir; my blood curdles to think of changing a single comma.

DE GUICHE. But when a verse pleases him, on the other hand, my dear, he pays well for it.

CYRANO. Not so well as I pay when I have made a verse which I love. I pay for it by singing it to myself!

DE GUICHE. You are proud.

CYRANO. Really, you have noticed it?

A CADET (*entering with his sword strung with hats, their feathers drooping, their crowns knocked in and full of holes*). Look, Cyrano, at the strange feathered game we took on the quay this morning! The hats of the fugitives!

CARBON. Opima spolia!

(*Everybody laughs! Ha! Ha! Ha!*)

CUIGY. Faith, whoever posted those rascals must be raging to-day.

BRISSAILLE. Does any one know who it was?

DE GUICHE. It was I. (*The laughter ceases.*) I charged them to chastise a drunken rhymester—a task one does not undertake one's self.

(*Awkward silence.*)

THE CADET (*in an undertone to Cyrano, pointing to the hats*). What is to be done with them? They are rich—a ragoût?

CYRANO (*taking the sword on which they are strung and making them, at one fell swoop, slide off at De Guiche's feet*). Sir, would you like to return them to your friends?

DE GUICHE (*rising and speaking shortly*). My chair and my porters at once: I am ready. (*To Cyrano, violently*). You, sir!—

A VOICE (*calling in the street*). The porters of my lord, the Count de Guiche!

DE GUICHE (*recovering his self-control with a smile*). Have you read "Don Quixote"?

CYRANO. I have read it, and take off my hat to that hair-brained fellow.

DE GUICHE. Be so good then as to consider—

A PORTER (*appearing at the back*). Here is the chair.

DE GUICHE. The chapter about the wind-mills!

CYRANO (*bowing*). Chapter thirteen.

DE GUICHE. For when one attacks them it often happens—

CYRANO. Am I attacking people who turn with every breeze?

DE GUICHE. That a windmill with its long canvas-covered arms hurls you into the mud!

CYRANO. Or rather among the stars!

(DE GUICHE *goes out. He is seen getting into his chair. The lords go away whispering.* LE BRET *accompanies them. The* Crowd *scatters.*)

SCENE EIGHTH

CYRANO, LE BRET, *the* Cadets, *seated at tables on the right and on the left and being served with refreshments.*

CYRANO (*bowing with a jeering air to those who are going out without venturing to bow to him*). Gentlemen—Gentlemen—Gentlemen—

LE BRET (*returning, holding up his arms in despair*). Ah! what pretty clothes.

CYRANO. Oh! you grumbler!

LE BRET. At last you will admit that murdering every passing chance becomes exaggerated.

CYRANO. Well, yes, I exaggerate!

LE BRET (*triumphant*). Ah!

CYRANO. But for the sake of principle, and for example, too, I find that it is a good thing to exaggerate thus.

LE BRET. If you relaxed your musketeer soul a little, fortune and glory—

CYRANO. What should I need to do? Seek a mighty protector, take a patron, and, like an obscure ivy twining around the trunk of a tree, procure myself a guardian by licking the bark, climb by trickery instead of rising by force? No, thank you. Be like all the rest and dedicate my verses to men of wealth? Change to a buffoon in the vile hope of seeing a favorable smile rise to some minister's lips? No, thank you! Breakfast every day on toads? Have my belly worn out with crawling? A skin quickly soiled about the knees? Execute tricks of dorsal agility? No, thank you! With one hand caress the hare while the other urges on the hounds, and give senna through desire for rhubarb, always to be burning incense in some one's face? No, thank you! To push from step to step, become a little great man in a ring, and sail, with madrigals for oars and elderly ladies' sighs to fill the sails? No, thank you! Pay the good publisher De Sercy to bring out my poems? No, thank you! To get named pope by the councils held by idiots in the wine-shops? No, thank you! To labor to make a name from one sonnet instead of making others? No, thank you! To show your talent only to novices? To be terrorized by vagrant journals, and to say continually, "Oh, if my name only appears in the sheets to the *Mercure François!*" No, thank you! To calculate, to be afraid, to grow pale, to prefer to make a call rather than write a poem, to frame petitions, to be introduced? No, thank you! no, thank you! no, thank you! But— to sing, to dream, to laugh, to pass along, to be alone, to be free, to have an accurate eye, a vibrating voice, to put my hat on awry when I please, to fight for a yes or a no—or to write a verse! To work without thought of glory or fortune on an imaginary journey to the moon! Never to write anything that does not proceed from the heart, and, moreover, to say modestly to myself, "My dear, be content with flowers, with fruits, even with leaves, if you gather them in your own garden!" Then if perchance a little success happens to come, not to be obliged to render any of it to Cæsar, but keep the merit all myself,—in short, scorn to be the parasitic ivy even if I am neither an oak nor a linden,—not to climb very high perhaps, but to climb all alone!

LE BRET. All alone, so be it! but not against all! How the devil have you contracted the frightful mania of always and everywhere making enemies?

CYRANO. From seeing you make friends and laugh at these friends of whom you have such multitudes, with lips full of scorn! I like to make greetings scarce along my path, and I exclaim with delight: One enemy more!

LE BRET. What a mistake!

CYRANO. Well! yes, that is my vice. To displease is my pleasure. I like to be hated. My dear, if you knew how much better it is to march under the exciting fire of angry eyes! What amusing spots the gall of the envious and the slobber of cowards make on one's doublet! The soft friendship with which you surround yourself resembles those great floating Italian collars of openwork, in which your neck grows weak; you feel more at ease in them, and less haughty, because, having neither support nor aid, your head is left to bend in every direction. But for my part, hatred every day lends me a fluted ruff, the starch of which compels me to hold up my head; each added enemy is a new plait, adding both a constraint and a ray of light, because, like the Spanish ruff in every respect, hatred is a pillory, but it is a halo of glory!

LE BRET (*after a silence, putting his arm under Cyrano's*). Openly be proud and bitter, but secretly tell me simply that she does not love thee!

CYRANO (*quickly*). Be still!

(*A moment before,* CHRISTIAN *has entered and mingled with the* Cadets, *who do not speak to him; he finally sits down alone at a little table, where* LISE *waits upon him.*)

SCENE NINTH

CYRANO, LE BRET, *the* Cadets, CHRISTIAN DE NEUVILLETTE

A CADET (*seated at a table at the back, a glass in his hand*). Hallo! Cyrano! (*Cyrano turns around.*) The story.

CYRANO. By and by!

(*He goes back on* LE BRET's *arm. They talk low.*)

THE CADET (*rising and coming forward*). The story of the combat! It will be the best lesson (*he stops in front of the table where Christian is*) for this timid recruit.

CHRISTIAN (*raising his head*). Recruit?

ANOTHER CADET. Yes, sickly northerner!

CHRISTIAN. Sickly?

FIRST CADET (*jeering*). Monsieur de Neuvillette, learn one thing: there is a subject which we never mention among us, any more than rope in the house of a man who has been hanged!

CHRISTIAN. What is it?

ANOTHER CADET (*in a terrible voice*). Look at me. (*He places his finger mysteriously on his nose three times.*) Do you understand me?

CHRISTIAN. Oh! it is—

ANOTHER. Hush! That word must never be spoken (*he points at Cyrano, who is talking at the back of stage with Le Bret*), or you will have to answer for it to him over there!

ANOTHER (*who, while he was turned toward the first, came and quietly seated himself on the table behind him*). Two snufflers were exterminated by him because they displeased him by talking through their noses!

ANOTHER (*in a hollow voice, rising from under the table, where he has crept on all fours*). You cannot make the least allusion to the fatal cartilage, without dying before your time!

ANOTHER (*placing his hand on his shoulder*). A word is enough! What do I say—a word? A single gesture! And to take out your handkerchief is to take out your winding-sheet!

(*Silence. All around with folded arms look at him. He rises
and goes to* CARBON DE CASTEL-JALOUX, *who is talking with an*
Officer *and seems to see no one.*)

CHRISTIAN. Captain!

CARBON (*turning around and looking at him from head to
foot*). Sir?

CHRISTIAN. What is to be done, when the southerners become
too boastful?

CARBON. Prove to them that a man may come from the North
and yet be courageous!

(*He turns his back.*)

CHRISTIAN. Thank you!

FIRST CADET (*to Cyrano*). Now for your story!

ALL. The story!

CYRANO (*coming toward them*). My story?

(*All draw up their stools, and group themselves around him,
stretching out their necks.* CHRISTIAN *sits astride a chair.*)

Well, then, I marched all alone to meet them. The moon
in the heavens shone like a watch, when suddenly some
strangely careful watchmaker began to draw a piece of cloudy
cotton over the silver case of this round watch, and it became
the darkest night in the world, and as the quays were not
illumined, 'Sdeath! you could not see farther—

CHRISTIAN. Than your nose.

(*Silence. Everybody rises slowly. They look at* CYRANO *in
alarm. The latter stops in amazement. Pause.*)

CYRANO. Who is that man there?

A CADET (*in a low voice*). He is a man who came in this
morning.

CYRANO (*taking a step toward Christian*). This morning?

CARBON (*in a low voice*). He is called the Baron de Neuvil—

CYRANO (*quickly, checking himself*). Ah! very well— (*He
turns pale, then red, and starts again to throw himself upon
Christian.*) I— (*Then he controls himself and says in a hollow
voice:*) Very well— (*He continues.*) I was saying— (*With a
burst of rage in his voice.*) 'Sdeath!— (*He goes on in a natural*

voice.) that nothing could be seen. (*Amazement. They sit down again, while watching him*.) And I marched on, thinking that for a very slender beggar I was going to displease some great person, some prince, who would surely have me—

CHRISTIAN. By the nose—

(*Everybody rises.* CHRISTIAN *sways back and forth in his chair.*)

CYRANO (*in a choking voice*). A tooth—for a tooth—and, in short, that I should imprudently thrust—

CHRISTIAN. Your nose—

CYRANO. My finger—between the bark and the tree, because this great person might be strong enough to hit me—

CHRISTIAN. On the nose—

CYRANO (*wiping the perspiration from his brow*). On the fingers. But I added: "March on, Gascon, do your duty! Go on, Cyrano!" And saying this, I ventured forth, when, in the darkness, some one gave me—

CHRISTIAN. A blow on the nose.

CYRANO. I parried it. And suddenly found myself—

CHRISTIAN. Nose to nose—

CYRANO (*leaping toward him with an oath*). (*All the Gascons rush to see; on reaching Christian, he controls himself and continues:*) With a hundred drunken brawlers, smelling—

CHRISTIAN. Enough to make you hold your nose.

CYRANO (*pale and smiling*). Of onions and bad wine! I leap forward, my head down—

CHRISTIAN. Nose in the air!

CYRANO. And I charge! I rip open two of them! I empale another there, as he stands. Some one aims at me: Paf! and I reply—

CHRISTIAN. Pif!

CYRANO (*bursting forth*). Thunder! Go out, all of you!

(*All the* Cadets *rush toward the doors.*)

FIRST CADET. The tiger is aroused!

CYRANO. All of you! And leave me alone with this man.

SECOND CADET. Heavens! We shall find him in mince-meat!

RAGUENEAU. In mince-meat!

ANOTHER CADET. In one of your pies!

RAGUENEAU. I feel pale, and as weak as a napkin!

CARBON. Let us go out!

ANOTHER. He will not leave a crumb of him.

ANOTHER. I am frightened to death to think of what is going to happen!

ANOTHER (*closing the door on the right*). 'Tis something terrible!

(*They all go out—some at the back, some at the sides, some have disappeared by the staircase.* CYRANO *and* CHRISTIAN *remain face to face and look at each other for a moment.*)

SCENE TENTH

CYRANO, CHRISTIAN

CYRANO. Embrace me!

CHRISTIAN. Sir—

CYRANO. Brave man.

CHRISTIAN. Ah! But!—

CYRANO. Very brave. I like you.

CHRISTIAN. What have you to say to me?

CYRANO. Embrace me. I am her brother.

CHRISTIAN. Whose?

CYRANO. Why, hers!

CHRISTIAN. What?

CYRANO. Why, Roxane's.

CHRISTIAN (*running toward him*). Heavens! You, her brother?

CYRANO. Or just the same, a brotherly cousin.

CHRISTIAN. She has told you?

CYRANO. Everything!

CHRISTIAN. Does she love me?

CYRANO. Perhaps so!

CHRISTIAN (*taking his hands*). How happy I am, sir, to know you!

CYRANO. This is what might be called a sudden sentiment.

CHRISTIAN. Pardon me—

CYRANO (*looking at him, and putting his hand on his shoulder*). It is true that he is handsome, the beggar!

CHRISTIAN. If you knew, sir, how I admire you!

CYRANO. But all those remarks you have made about noses—

CHRISTIAN. I take them back!

CYRANO. Roxane expects a letter to-night—

CHRISTIAN. Alas!

CYRANO. What?

CHRISTIAN. I am lost, unless I keep quiet!

CYRANO. How is that?

CHRISTIAN. Alas! I am so stupid that I could kill myself for shame.

CYRANO. No, you are not, because you recognize the fact. Besides, you did not attack me stupidly.

CHRISTIAN. Bah! One finds words when one mounts to the assault! Yes, I have a certain easy, soldierly wit, but before women I can only keep silent. Oh! Their eyes are kindly disposed toward me as I pass—

CYRANO. Are not their hearts more so when you stop?

CHRISTIAN. No! for I am one of those—I know it—and I tremble to think of it!—who are unable to talk of love.

CYRANO. Wait! It seems to me that if care had been taken to model me better, I should have been one of those who would be able to talk of it.

CHRISTIAN. Oh! to be able to express things gracefully!

CYRANO. To be a handsome little musketeer!

CHRISTIAN. Roxane is fastidious, and I shall surely disappoint her!

CYRANO (*looking at Christian*). If I had such an interpreter to express my soul!

CHRISTIAN (*with despair*). I need eloquence!

CYRANO (*abruptly*). I will lend it to you! You lend me your conquering, physical charms, and together let us make a hero of romance!

CHRISTIAN. What?

CYRANO. Could you repeat the things that I would teach you each day?

CHRISTIAN. What are you proposing to me?

CYRANO. Roxane shall never be undeceived. Tell me, if together we two shall try to charm her? Are you willing to feel the soul, which I breathe into you, pass from my leather jerkin to your embroidered doublet?

CHRISTIAN. But, Cyrano!—

CYRANO. Christian, are you willing?

CHRISTIAN. You frighten me!

CYRANO. Since you are afraid, alone, of making her heart turn cold, are you willing to let your lips coöperate with my phrases —and soon her heart shall be on fire?

CHRISTIAN. How your eyes shine!

CYRANO. Are you willing?

CHRISTIAN. What! Would it give you so much pleasure?

CYRANO (*carried away*). This— (*Correcting himself, and speaking like an artist.*) This would amuse me! It is an experience which tempts a poet. Are you willing to complete me, and to let me complete you? You shall go forward, I will be in the shadow at your side: I will be your wit, you shall be my beauty.

CHRISTIAN. But the letter which ought to be sent her at once! I could never—

CYRANO (*taking from his doublet the letter he has written*). Wait, here is your letter!

CHRISTIAN. What?

CYRANO. Nothing is lacking, except the signature.

CHRISTIAN. I—

CYRANO. You can send it. Be calm. It is all right.

CHRISTIAN. You had it?

CYRANO. We always have epistles to our Chlorises in our pockets—written out of our heads, because we have for sweethearts only dreams blown into the bubble of a name! Take it, and change pretences to truths; these confessions and complaints I shot at random: you shall make all these vagrant birds alight. You will see that in this letter—take it!—I was the more eloquent because I was less sincere! So take it, and have done with it!

CHRISTIAN. Is it not necessary to change some of the words? Written haphazard, will it fit Roxane?

CYRANO. It will fit her like a glove!

CHRISTIAN. But—

CYRANO. The credulity of self-love is such that Roxane will believe that it was written for her!

CHRISTIAN. Ah! my friend!

(*He throws himself into* CYRANO's *arms. They remain in an embrace.*)

SCENE ELEVENTH

CYRANO, CHRISTIAN, *the* Gascons, *the* Musketeer, LISE.

A CADET (*opening the door*). Not a sound—a deathly silence —I dare not look— (*He puts in his head*). What?

ALL THE CADETS (*entering and seeing Cyrano and Christian embracing each other*). Ah!—Oh!—

A CADET. This is too much!

(*Consternation.*)

THE MUSKETEER (*jeering*). Indeed?

CARBON. Our demon is gentle as an apostle, is he? When one smites him on one nostril,—does he offer the other?

THE MUSKETEER. So we can speak about his nose, now? (*Calling Lise with a triumphant air.*) Eh! Lise! You will see! (*Sniffing the air with affectation.*) Oh!—oh!—it is surprising! What an odor! (*Going to Cyrano.*) You, sir, must have noticed it? What does it smell of here?

CYRANO (*slapping his face*). A buffet!

(*Delight. The* Cadets *have found* CYRANO *again; they turn somersaults. Curtain falls.*)

94

ACT THIRD

ROXANE'S KISS.

A small square in the old Marais. Ancient houses. Vistas of lanes. On the right, ROXANE'S *house and her garden wall overhung with thick foliage. Above the door a window and a balcony. A seat in front of the door.*

Ivy climbs over the wall, the balcony is festooned with jasmine which climbs up and falls back.

One can easily mount to the balcony by the seat and the stones projecting from the wall.

Opposite, an old house in the same style, of brick and stone, with an entrance door. The knocker on this door is wound with linen like a bruised thumb.

When the curtain rises, the Duenna *is seated on the bench. The window is wide open on* ROXANE'S *balcony.*

Near the Duenna *stands* RAGUENEAU, *dressed in a sort of livery; he is finishing a story, wiping his eyes.*

∞∞∞∞∞∞∞∞∞∞∞∞∞∞∞∞∞∞∞∞∞∞∞∞∞

SCENE FIRST

RAGUENEAU, *the* Duenna, *then* ROXANE, CYRANO, *and two* Pages

RAGUENEAU. And then she went off with a musketeer! Alone, ruined, I am hanging myself. I have left this earth. Monsieur de Bergerac comes in, and taking me down offers me to his cousin as a steward.

THE DUENNA. But how do you explain this ruinous state of affairs?

RAGUENEAU. Lise loved warriors, and I loved poets. Mars ate the cakes which Apollo left. Then, you understand it was not long!

THE DUENNA (*rising and calling up to the open window*). Roxane, are you ready? They are waiting for us!

ROXANE's VOICE (*from the window*). I am putting on my cloak!

THE DUENNA (*to Ragueneau, pointing to the door opposite*). They are expecting us over there, at Clomire's house. She is holding a meeting at her retreat. To-day some one reads a discourse on the Tender Passion.

RAGUENEAU. On the Tender Passion?

THE DUENNA (*simpering*). Why, yes! (*Calling toward the window.*) Roxane, you must come down, or we shall lose the discourse on the Tender Passion.

ROXANE's VOICE. I am coming!

(*The sound of stringed instruments is heard approaching.*)

CYRANO's VOICE (*singing in the side-scenes*). La! la! la! la!

THE DUENNA (*in surprise*). Is some one going to serenade us?

CYRANO (*followed by two Pages carrying lutes*). I tell you that is a demi-semi-quaver, you demi-semi-fool.

FIRST PAGE (*ironically*). You know then, sir, that they are demi-semi-quavers?

CYRANO. I am a musician, like all the disciples of Gassendi!

THE PAGE (*playing and singing*). La! la!

CYRANO (*snatching the lute from him and continuing the musical phrase*). I can go on! La! la! la! la!

ROXANE (*appearing on the balcony*). Is it you?

CYRANO (*singing to the air which he keeps up*). I, who come to greet your lilies and pay my respects to your ro—ses!

ROXANE. I am coming down!

(*She leaves the balcony.*)

THE DUENNA (*pointing to the Pages*). Who are those two virtuosos?

CYRANO. They are a wager I won from D'Assoucy. We were discussing a point of grammar, when suddenly pointing to those two great gawks, skilled in scraping the strings with their claws, and whom he always takes about with him as escort, he said: "I wager you a day of music!" He lost. So until Phœbus begins his course again I have these lute-players at my heels, harmonious witnesses of everything I do! At first it was delightful, and now it is not so much so. (*To the Musicians.*) Hep! Go play a pavan to Montfleury for me! (*The Pages go to the back of the stage to go out. To the Duenna.*) I come to ask Roxane, as I do every night— (*To the Pages, who are going out.*) Play a long time—and out of tune! (*To the Duenna.*) Whether the friend of her soul is still faultless?

ROXANE (*coming out of the house*). Ah! how handsome he is, how witty, and how I love him!

CYRANO (*smiling*). Christian is so witty?

ROXANE. My dear, even more so than yourself!

CYRANO. I admit it.

ROXANE. To my mind no one exists who can say the pretty nothings which are everything, as delicately as he. Sometimes he is absent-minded, his muse wanders, then suddenly he says the most delightful things!

CYRANO (*incredulously*). No!

ROXANE. It is too much! This is what men are; if they are handsome they will not be witty!

CYRANO. Does he speak skilfully from the heart?

ROXANE. He does not speak, sir; he discourses!

CYRANO. Does he write you?

ROXANE. Better still! Listen for a moment. (*Declaiming:*) "The more of my heart you take away, the more I have left!" (*Triumphantly to Cyrano.*) Isn't that good?

CYRANO. Pooh!

ROXANE. And this: "Since I must have another, in order to feel, if you keep my heart, send me yours!"

CYRANO. Sometimes he has too much, sometimes not enough. Just how much heart does he wish?

ROXANE. You are teasing me! It is jealousy—

CYRANO (*starting*). What?

ROXANE. Of the author which is devouring you! And this— isn't it tender to the last degree? "Believe that toward you my heart makes but one cry, and if kisses could be sent by writing, madame, you would read my letter with your lips!"

CYRANO (*smiling with satisfaction, in spite of himself*). Ha! ha! these lines are—well! well! (*correcting himself, and with scorn*) very cunning!

ROXANE. And this—

CYRANO (*delighted*). You know his letters, then, by heart?

ROXANE. Every one!

CYRANO. There's nothing to say; he is a flatterer!

ROXANE. He is a master!

CYRANO (*modestly*). Oh!—a master!

ROXANE (*peremptorily*). A master!

CYRANO. So be it! A master!

THE DUENNA (*who had gone to the back of the stage, coming forward in haste*). Monsieur de Guiche! (*To Cyrano, pushing him toward the house.*) Go into the house! For it will be better, perhaps, if he does not find you here; it might make him suspicious—

ROXANE. Yes, of my dear secret! He is in love with me, he

is powerful, he must not know! He might give my love a severe blow.

CYRANO (*going into the house*). Well! well! well!

(DE GUICHE *appears*.)

SCENE SECOND

ROXANE, DE GUICHE, *the* Duenna *at a distance*

ROXANE (*to De Guiche, making him a courtesy*). I was going out.

DE GUICHE. I have come to say farewell.

ROXANE. Are you going away?

DE GUICHE. To war.

ROXANE. Ah!

DE GUICHE. This very night.

ROXANE. Ah!

DE GUICHE. I have orders. Arras is besieged.

ROXANE. Ah! besieged?

DE GUICHE. Yes. My departure seems to fill your atmosphere with snow.

ROXANE. Oh!

DE GUICHE. I am grieved. Shall I ever see you again? When? You know that I have been named commander?

ROXANE (*indifferently*). Bravo!

DE GUICHE. Of the regiment of the guards.

ROXANE (*startled*). Ah? Of the guards?

DE GUICHE. The same in which your cousin serves, the man of boastful words. I shall find a way to avenge myself on him out there.

ROXANE (*choking*). What! Are the guards going there?

DE GUICHE (*laughing*). Wait! that is my regiment!

ROXANE (*dropping on the bench, aside*). Christian!

DE GUICHE. What is the matter?

ROXANE (*very much moved*). This—departure—fills me with despair. To know that one I care for has gone to war!

DE GUICHE (*surprised and delighted*). For the first time, on the day of my departure you speak a tender word to me!

ROXANE (*changing her tone and fanning herself*). Then—are you going to avenge yourself on my cousin?

DE GUICHE (*smiling*). Are you for him?

ROXANE. No—against him!

DE GUICHE. Do you ever see him?

ROXANE. Very seldom.

DE GUICHE. One meets him everywhere with one of the cadets (*he tries to think of the name*)—that Neu—villen—viller—

ROXANE. A tall man!

DE GUICHE. Light.

ROXANE. Sandy.

DE GUICHE. Handsome!

ROXANE. Pooh!

DE GUICHE. But stupid.

ROXANE. He looks so! (*Changing her tone.*) Your vengeance toward Cyrano,—is perhaps to expose him to fire, which he adores? A sorry vengeance! But I know what would be galling to him!

DE GUICHE. It is?

ROXANE. When the regiment starts away, if it should leave him and his dear cadets with folded arms in Paris during the entire war! That is the only way to enrage a man like him; do you wish to punish him?—deprive him of danger.

DE GUICHE. A woman! a woman! Only a woman could invent such a trick!

ROXANE. He would eat his soul out, and his friends gnaw their fists, not to be in the thick of the fire: and you would be avenged!

DE GUICHE (*approaching her*). Do you love me a little, then? (*She smiles.*) In thus espousing my rancor, I should like to see a proof of love, Roxane!

ROXANE. It is one.

DE GUICHE (*showing several sealed letters*). I have orders with me which are to be given to each company at once, except (*he separates one*) this one! This is for the cadets. (*He puts it in his pocket.*) I will keep it. (*Laughing.*) Ha! Ha! Ha! Cyrano! His fancy for battles! So even you play tricks on people?

ROXANE. Sometimes.

DE GUICHE (*very near her*). You infatuate me! To-night—listen—yes, I ought to leave. But how go away when I feel that you are touched! Listen. Near here, in the Rue d'Orléans, there is a convent founded by the syndic of the Capuchin monks, Père Athanase. A layman cannot enter there. But I know how to manage the good Fathers! They can hide me in their sleeve; it is large enough. They are the Capuchins who serve Richelieu at home; dreading the uncle, they fear the nephew. It will be believed that I have gone. I will come masked. Let me stay behind one day, dear capricious one!

ROXANE. But if that be known, your glory—

DE GUICHE. Bah!

ROXANE. But the siege at Arras—

DE GUICHE. So much the worse! Let me stay!

ROXANE. No!

DE GUICHE. Allow me!

ROXANE (*tenderly*). I must forbid it!

DE GUICHE. Ah!

ROXANE. Go! (*Aside.*) Christian will remain. (*Aloud.*) I wish you to be heroic,—Antoine!

DE GUICHE. Heavenly word! You love it, then?

ROXANE. It has made me tremble.

DE GUICHE (*carried away with delight*). Ah! I am going! (*He kisses her hand.*) Are you happy?

ROXANE. Yes, my friend! (*He goes out.*)

THE DUENNA (*making a comical courtesy behind him*). Yes, my friend!

ROXANE (*to the Duenna*). Say nothing of what I have just

done! Cyrano will be angry with me for robbing him of his war! (*She calls toward the house.*) Cousin!

SCENE THIRD

ROXANE, *the* Duenna, CYRANO

ROXANE. We will go to Clomire's house. (*She designates the door opposite.*) Alcandre is to speak there, and Lysimon!

THE DUENNA (*putting her little finger in her ear*). Yes! but my little finger says that we shall miss them!

CYRANO (*to Roxane*). Don't miss those monkeys.

(*They reach* CLOMIRE's *door.*)

THE DUENNA (*with delight*). Oh! see! the knocker is wound with linen! (*To the knocker.*) You have been gagged so that your metal may not disturb the fine discourses,—little brute!

(*She raises it with infinite care and knocks gently.*)

ROXANE (*seeing the door open*). Let us go in! (*From the threshold, to Cyrano.*) If Christian comes, as I presume he will, let him wait for me!

CYRANO (*quickly, just as she is disappearing*). Ah! (*She turns around.*) What are you going to ask him about, to-day, according to your custom?

ROXANE. About—

CYRANO (*quickly*). About?—

ROXANE. But you must keep silent about it!

CYRANO. Silent as a wall.

ROXANE. About nothing! I am going to say to him: Go on! Let yourself out! Improvise. Talk of love. Be brilliant!

CYRANO (*smiling*). Good.

ROXANE. Hush!

CYRANO. Hush!

ROXANE. Not a word!

(*She goes in and closes the door.*)

CYRANO (*bowing to her, as soon as the door is closed*). Thank you!

(*The door opens again and* ROXANE *puts out her head.*)

ROXANE. He would be prepared!

CYRANO. The devil, no!

BOTH (*together*). Hush!

(*The door closes.*)

CYRANO (*calling*). Christian.

SCENE FOURTH

CYRANO, CHRISTIAN

CYRANO. I know all about it! Prepare your memory. Here is an opportunity to cover yourself with glory. Let us lose no time. Don't look so unhappy. Quick, let us return to your house, for I am going to teach you—

CHRISTIAN. No!

CYRANO. What?

CHRISTIAN. No! I will wait for Roxane here.

CYRANO. What has turned your head? Come learn quickly—

CHRISTIAN. No, I tell you! I am tired of borrowing my letters and my conversation, of playing this rôle and trembling all the while! It was good at first! But I feel that she loves me! Thank you. I am no longer afraid. I am going to speak myself.

CYRANO. Indeed!

CHRISTIAN. Who told you that I should not know how? At last I am not so stupid! You shall see! But, my dear, your lessons have been profitable. I shall know how to speak alone! And, by all the devils, I shall know very well how to take her in my arms! (*Seeing Roxane as she comes out of Clomire's house.*) 'Tis she! Cyrano, no, do not leave me!

CYRANO (*bowing to him*). Speak by yourself, sir.

(*He disappears behind the garden wall.*)

SCENE FIFTH

CHRISTIAN, ROXANE, *the* Duenna *for a moment*

ROXANE (*coming out of Clomire's house with others whom she is leaving; courtesies and bows*). Barthénoïde! Alcandre! Grémione!

THE DUENNA (*in despair*). We have missed the discourse on the Tender Passion!

(*She goes into* ROXANE's *house.*)

ROXANE (*bowing again*). Urimédonte! Farewell! (*All bow to Roxane, bow again to one another, separate and go away by different streets. Roxane sees Christian.*) 'Tis you! (*She goes to him.*) Night is falling. Wait. They have gone. The air is mild. No one is passing. Let us sit down. Talk. I am listening.

CHRISTIAN (*sits down near her, on the seat. Silence*). I love you.

ROXANE (*closing her eyes*). Yes, talk to me of love.

CHRISTIAN. I love thee.

ROXANE. That is the theme. Embroider it, embroider it.

CHRISTIAN. I love—

ROXANE. Embroider it!

CHRISTIAN. I love thee so much!

ROXANE. Without doubt, and what then?

CHRISTIAN. And then—I should be so happy if you loved me! Tell me, Roxane, that thou lovest me!

ROXANE (*pouting*). You offer me gruel when I hoped for creams! Tell me a little how you love me!

CHRISTIAN. Why—very much.

ROXANE. Oh! Diselabyrinth your sentiments!

CHRISTIAN. Thy neck! I wish I could kiss it!

ROXANE. Christian!

CHRISTIAN. I love thee!

ROXANE (*starting to rise*). Again!

CHRISTIAN (*quickly, detaining her*). No! I do not love thee!

ROXANE (*sitting down again*). That is fortunate!

CHRISTIAN. I adore thee!

ROXANE (*rising and moving away*). Oh!

CHRISTIAN. Yes—I am growing stupid!

ROXANE (*dryly*). And that displeases me as much as if you should become ugly.

CHRISTIAN. But—

ROXANE. Go chase your escaping eloquence!

CHRISTIAN. I—

ROXANE. You love me, I know. Farewell.

(*She goes toward the house.*)

CHRISTIAN. Not so soon! I will tell you—

ROXANE (*pushing the door to go in*). How you adore me—yes, I know. No! No! Go away!

CHRISTIAN. But I—

(*She shuts the door in his face.*)

CYRANO (*who has just entered without being seen*). It is a success.

SCENE SIXTH

CHRISTIAN, CYRANO, *the* Pages *for a moment*

CHRISTIAN. Help me!

CYRANO. No, sir.

CHRISTIAN. I shall die if I cannot get back into her good graces, this very instant.

CYRANO. And how the deuce can I teach you this very instant?

CHRISTIAN (*seizing his arm*). Oh! there, wait, see!

(*The window on the balcony is lighted up.*)

CYRANO (*moved*). Her window!

CHRISTIAN. I shall die!

CYRANO. Lower your voice!

CHRISTIAN (*very low*). Die! I shall die!

CYRANO. It is a dark night!

CHRISTIAN. Well?

CYRANO. It can be atoned for, but you don't deserve it. Stand there, wretch! There in front of the balcony! I will take my place underneath—and I will whisper your words to you.

CHRISTIAN. But—

CYRANO. Be still!

THE PAGES (*appearing at the back, to Cyrano*). Hep!

CYRANO. Hush!

(*He signs to them to speak low.*)

FIRST PAGE (*in a low voice*). We have just given the serenade to Montfleury!

CYRANO (*low, quickly*). Go lie in wait, one at this corner of the street, the other at that; and if any inconvenient passer-by comes this way, play a tune!

SECOND PAGE. What kind of a tune, oh, follower of Gassendi?

CYRANO. A merry one for a woman, and a sad one for a man! (*The Pages disappear, one to each corner of the street. To Christian.*) Call her!

CHRISTIAN. Roxane!

CYRANO (*picking up some pebbles, which he throws against the window*). Wait! Here are some pebbles.

ROXANE (*opening her window a little way*). Who is calling me?

CHRISTIAN. I am.

ROXANE. Who is "I"?

CHRISTIAN. Christian.

ROXANE (*disdainfully*). It is you?

CHRISTIAN. I wish to speak to you.

CYRANO (*under the balcony, to Christian*). Good. Good. Almost whisper.

ROXANE. No! Your speech is too awkward. Go away!

CHRISTIAN. Forgive me!—

ROXANE. No! you no longer love me!

CHRISTIAN (*to whom Cyrano whispers what he is to say*). Accuse me—righteous heavens!—of loving you no longer— when—I love you so much more!

ROXANE (*stopping just as she was about to close her window*). Ah! That is better!

CHRISTIAN (*same action*). Love grows, rocked in my restless soul, which this cruel boy takes for his cradle!

ROXANE (*coming forward on the balcony*). That is better! But since this love is cruel, you were foolish not to stifle it in the cradle!

CHRISTIAN (*the same action*). I have tried it, but—all in vain; this—new-born infant, madame, is a little—Hercules.

ROXANE. That is better!

CHRISTIAN (*the same action*). So that it—strangles as if they were nothing—the two serpents—Pride and—Doubt.

ROXANE (*resting her elbows on the balcony*). Ah! That is very good! But why do you speak so hesitatingly? Have you the gout in your imagination?

CYRANO (*drawing Christian under the balcony, and gliding into his place*). Hush! This is growing too difficult!

ROXANE. To-day your words are halting. Why is it?

CYRANO (*speaking low like Christian*). It is because it is night. Groping about in this darkness, they are trying to find your ear.

ROXANE. Mine experience no such difficulty.

CYRANO. They find their way at once? Oh, that is easy, since I receive them into my heart; now my heart is large while your ear is small. Besides your words descend: they move quickly. Mine rise, madame: they need more time!

ROXANE. They rise much better in the last few moments.

CYRANO. They are getting accustomed to the exercise!

ROXANE. I am speaking to you, indeed, from a real height!

CYRANO. Surely and you would kill me if from that height you should drop a single hard word upon my heart!

ROXANE (*moving*). I am coming down.

CYRANO (*quickly*). No!

ROXANE (*pointing to the seat under the balcony*). Climb up on the seat then, quickly!

CYRANO (*drawing back, in alarm, into the darkness*). No!

ROXANE. Why not?

CYRANO (*whose emotion is increasing more and more*). Let us take advantage of this opportunity to be able to speak together softly without seeing each other.

ROXANE. Without seeing each other?

CYRANO. Why, yes; it is heavenly. We can hardly make each other out. You see the blackness of a long trailing cloak. I distinguish the whiteness of a summer gown: I am only a shadow, and you only a gleam of light! You have no idea what these moments mean to me! If sometimes I have been eloquent—

ROXANE. You have been!

CYRANO. Never has my language until now come from my real heart.

ROXANE. Why?

CYRANO. Because—till now, I spoke through—

ROXANE. What?

CYRANO. The dizziness in which every one who comes under your eyes must tremble! But to-night it seems to me that I am speaking to you for the first time!

ROXANE. It is true that you have quite a different voice.

CYRANO (*drawing nearer, feverishly*). Yes, quite different, because in the protecting darkness I dare at last to be myself, and I dare— (*He stops, confused.*) Where was I? I do not know—all this—forgive my emotion—is so delicious—it is so new to me!

ROXANE. So new?

CYRANO (*distracted and still trying to collect his words*). So new—yes—to be sincere: the fear of being laughed at has always oppressed my heart.

ROXANE. Why laughed at?

CYRANO. Because of—of my impulsiveness! Yes, my heart always clothes itself with my wit, through modesty: I start out to unfasten a star, and I stop through fear of ridicule to gather a little flower!

ROXANE. There is some good in the little flower.

CYRANO. To-night let us disdain it!

ROXANE. You have never talked to me like that before.

CYRANO. Ah! so far from quivers, torches, and arrows, let us flee to other things—more refreshing! Instead of drinking the tasteless water of the Lignon drop by drop from a tiny golden thimble, let us try to see how the soul slakes its thirst by drinking as freely as possible of the great river!

ROXANE. But your wit?

CYRANO. I made use of it at first to hold you, but now it would be to insult this night, these perfumes, this hour, even Nature, to speak like one of Voiture's love letters! Let Heaven with a single look from her bright stars set us free from all that's artificial: I fear so much lest in the midst of our exquisite alchemy, true sentiment may vanish away like a vapor, that the soul may become empty with these idle pastimes, and the refinement of the fine be the final finality.

ROXANE. But your wit?

CYRANO. I hate it in love! It is a crime when in love to prolong this fencing unduly! Moreover, the moment comes inevitably,—and I pity those for whom it never comes,—when we feel that in us exists a love so noble that every trifling word we speak makes it melancholy.

ROXANE. Well! If this moment has come for us two, what kind of words would you speak to me?

CYRANO. All those, all those, all those which come to me, I am going to throw you in a bunch, without arranging them in a bouquet: I love you, I am stifling, I love thee, I am mad, I can say no more, it is too much; your name is like a bell in my heart, and as I tremble all the time, the bell is continually moving and the name ringing out! I remember everything about you, for I have loved everything! I know that one day last year, the twelfth of May, when you went out in the morning, your hair was dressed in a different fashion! Your hair had been to me such a shining light that just as after looking too long at the sun one sees crimson circles everywhere, so when I turned from your overwhelming blaze, my dazzled eyes met only golden clouds!

ROXANE (*in an agitated voice*). Yes, this is really love. . . .

CYRANO. Surely, this feeling which pervades me, so terrible and jealous, is truly love; it has all the melancholy madness of love—and yet it is not selfish! Ah! how gladly would I sacrifice my happiness for yours, even if you should never know anything about it, if it might happen sometimes that from afar I might hear the laughter of your gladness born of my self-sacrifice! Each look from you arouses new virtue, new valor in me! Are you beginning to understand now? Can you account for it? Do you feel my soul a little, as it climbs in the darkness? Oh! but truly, this night is far too beautiful, it is too sweet! I am telling you all this, you are listening to me, to me, you! It is too much! Even in my least modest dream I never have hoped for so much! Nothing is left for me now but to die! On account of the words I say she is trembling among the blue branches! For you are trembling like a leaf among leaves! You are trembling, because, whether you wished it or not, I felt the adorable thrill of your hand descend along the jasmine branches!

(*He passionately kisses the end of a hanging vine.*)

ROXANE. Yes, I am trembling and I am weeping, and I love thee, and I am thine! You have intoxicated me!

CYRANO. Then, let death come! It is I, it is I, who have been the cause of this intoxication! I only ask one thing more.

CHRISTIAN (*under the balcony*). A kiss!

ROXANE (*starting back*). What?

CYRANO. Oh!

ROXANE. You ask?

CYRANO. Yes—I— (*In a low voice to Christian.*) You are getting on too fast.

CHRISTIAN. Since she is so agitated, I must take advantage of it!

CYRANO (*to Roxane*). Yes I—I asked, it is true, but, righteous heavens, I understand that I was far too audacious.

ROXANE (*somewhat disappointed*). You no longer insist upon it?

CYRANO. Yes! I insist—without insisting! Yes, yes! your modesty is grieved! Well! but this kiss—do not grant it!

CHRISTIAN (*to Cyrano, pulling his cloak*). Why?

CYRANO. Be silent, Christian!

ROXANE (*leaning over*). What are you saying so low?

CYRANO. I was scolding myself for having gone too far; I was saying: be silent, Christian! (*The lutes begin to play.*) One moment! Some one is coming! (*Roxane closes the window. Cyrano listens to the lutes, one of which plays a merry tune and the other a melancholy air.*) A sad tune? A gay tune? What is their object? Is it a man? a woman?—Ah! It is a Capuchin!

(*A* Capuchin *monk enters and with a lantern in his hand goes from house to house, looking at the doors.*)

SCENE SEVENTH

CYRANO, CHRISTIAN, *a* Capuchin

CYRANO (*to the Capuchin*). Who's this new Diogenes?

THE CAPUCHIN. I am looking for the house of Madame . . .

CHRISTIAN. He is in our way!

THE CAPUCHIN. Magdeleine Robin . . .

CHRISTIAN. What does he want?

CYRANO (*showing him a street in the background*). That way! Straight ahead,—keep straight ahead—

THE CAPUCHIN. I am going to say—thank you!—my chaplet for you even to the Pater Noster.

CYRANO. Good luck to you! My good wishes follow your cowl!

(*He comes back to* CHRISTIAN.)

SCENE EIGHTH

CHRISTIAN. Get me that kiss!

CYRANO. No!

CHRISTIAN. Sooner or later—

CYRANO. That is true! That moment of dizzy intoxication when your lips will meet on account of her rosy mouth and your fair mustache! (*To himself*.) I should like it better if it were on account of—

(*Sound of shutters opening.* CHRISTIAN *hides under the balcony.*)

SCENE NINTH

CYRANO, CHRISTIAN, ROXANE

ROXANE (*coming forward on the balcony*). Is it you? We were speaking about—about—about a . . .

CYRANO. Kiss. The word is sweet. I do not see why your lips should not try it. If it burns them now, what will the actual experience be? Don't be alarmed. Did you not just now almost unconsciously stop jesting and pass fearlessly from a smile to a sigh, and from the sigh to tears? Pass on once more in somewhat the same unconscious fashion—from tears to a kiss is only a thrill!

ROXANE. Be still!

CYRANO. A kiss, when all is told, what is it? An oath taken a little closer, a promise more exact. A wish which longs to be confirmed, a rosy dot placed on the *i* in the participle loving; it is a secret which takes the lips for the ear, a moment of infinity humming like a bee, a communion tasting of flowers, a way of breathing in a little of the heart and tasting a little of the soul with the edge of the lips!

ROXANE. Be still!

CYRANO. A kiss is so noble, madame, that the queen of France, even the queen, allowed the happiest of lords to take one!

ROXANE. Forsooth!

CYRANO (*over-excited*). Like Buckingham I have suffered in silence, like him I adore the queen that you are, like him I am sad and faithful—

ROXANE. And like him you are handsome!

CYRANO (*aside, growing sober*). It is true, I am handsome, I was forgetting!

ROXANE. Well! climb up and gather this unequalled flower.

CYRANO (*pushing Christian toward the balcony*). Climb up!

ROXANE. This tasting of the heart—

CYRANO. Climb up!

ROXANE. This humming of a bee—

CYRANO. Climb up!

CHRISTIAN (*hesitating*). It seems to me, now, that it is the wrong time!

ROXANE. This moment of infinity!

CYRANO (*pushing him*). Climb up then, you animal!

CHRISTIAN (*darts forward and by means of the seat, the vines, and the posts reaches the railing, which he leaps over*). Ah! Roxane!

(*He throws his arms about her and bends over her lips.*)

CYRANO. Ah! What a strange pain in my heart! O kiss, feast of love, at which I am the Lazarus, a crumb of thee comes to me in the darkness—yes. I feel that my heart receives a little of thee, for on those lips whereto Roxane is lured, she is kissing the words that I have only just now spoken! (*The lutes are heard.*) A sad tune, a gay tune: the monk! (*He pretends to run as if he had come from a distance and speaking in a clear voice.*) Hallo!

ROXANE. Who is it?

CYRANO. I. I was passing by. Is Christian still there?

CHRISTIAN (*very much surprised*). What, Cyrano!

ROXANE. Good evening, cousin!

CYRANO. Good evening, cousin!

ROXANE. I am coming down!

(*She disappears into the house. The* Capuchin *enters at the back.*)

CHRISTIAN (*seeing him*). Oh! Again!

(*He follows* ROXANE.)

SCENE TENTH

CYRANO, CHRISTIAN, ROXANE, *the* Capuchin, RAGUENEAU

THE CAPUCHIN. It is here—I insist upon it—Magdeleine Robin!

CYRANO. You said: Ro-*lin*.

THE CAPUCHIN. No: *bin,* b, i, n, bin!

ROXANE (*appearing on the threshold, followed by Ragueneau carrying a lantern, and by Christian*). What is it?

THE CAPUCHIN. A letter.

CHRISTIAN. What?

THE CAPUCHIN (*to Roxane*). Oh! it can only concern some holy thing! A worthy lord—

ROXANE (*to Christian*). It is from De Guiche!

CHRISTIAN. Does he dare?

ROXANE. Oh! He is not going to trouble me always! (*Unsealing the letter.*) I love thee, and if— (*By the light of Ragueneau's lantern, she reads, apart, and in a low voice.*)

"MADEMOISELLE,—

The drums are beating; my men are putting on their regimentals; they are ready to start; they think that I have already gone; I am still here. I have disobeyed you. I am in this convent. I am on the point of coming, and send you word in advance by a monk as simple as a nanny-goat, who can understand nothing of this. Your lips smiled too sweetly on me just now; I long to see them again. Keep every one away and deign to receive the audacious suitor already pardoned, I hope, who signs himself your very—et cetera—."

(*To the Capuchin.*)
Here is what this letter says, Listen:—
(*All draw near; she reads aloud.*)

"MADEMOISELLE,—
The Cardinal's wishes must be carried out, however hard it may be for you. That is the reason why I have chosen a very holy, very intelligent and discreet Capuchin to place these lines in your charming hands; we desire him to give you the nuptial (*she turns over the page*) benediction, in your own home, at once. Christian is to become your husband secretly; I send him to you. It does not please you. Be resigned. Believe that Heaven will bless your zeal and be assured, mademoiselle, of the respect of one who has been and always will be your very humble and very—et cetera."

THE CAPUCHIN (*beaming*). The worthy lord! I said so. I was not afraid! It could only be some holy matter!

ROXANE (*in a low voice to Christian*). Don't I read letters very well?

CHRISTIAN. Humph!

ROXANE (*aloud, with despair*). Ah!—It is frightful!

THE CAPUCHIN (*having directed the light of his lantern toward Cyrano*). It's you, is it?

CHRISTIAN. It is I.

THE CAPUCHIN (*turning the light toward him, and as if a doubt occurred to him on noticing his beauty*). But—

ROXANE (*quickly*). Postscript:—

"Give one hundred and twenty pistoles for the convent."

THE CAPUCHIN. The worthy, worthy lord! (*To Roxane.*) Be resigned!

ROXANE (*with the air of a martyr*). I am resigned! (*While Ragueneau is opening the door to the Capuchin whom Christian invites to enter she speaks low to Cyrano*). Keep De Guiche here! He will soon be coming! Don't let him come in as long as—

CYRANO. I understand! (*To the Capuchin.*) How long will it take to bless them?

THE CAPUCHIN. A quarter of an hour.

CYRANO (*pushing them all toward the house*). Go in! I will stay here!

ROXANE (*to Christian*). Come!

(*They go in.*)

CYRANO. How shall I detain De Guiche for a quarter of an hour? (*He jumps on the bench and climbs on the wall toward the balcony.*) There! Let us climb up! I have a plan! (*The lutes begin to play a melancholy phrase.*) Ho! It is a man! (*The tremolo becomes tragic.*) Ho! Ho! This time, it is surely one! (*He is on the balcony; he pulls his hat down over his eyes, takes off his sword, wraps his cloak around him, then leans over and looks down.*) No, it is not too high! (*He strides the railing and drawing toward him a long branch of one of the trees growing beside the garden wall, he takes hold of it with both hands, ready to let himself drop.*) I am going to make a slight disturbance in this atmosphere!

SCENE ELEVENTH

CYRANO, DE GUICHE

DE GUICHE (*entering, masked, feeling his way in the darkness*). What can that cursed Capuchin be doing?

CYRANO. The devil! my voice? If he should recognize it? (*Letting go with one hand, he seems to be turning an invisible key.*) Crick! Crack! (*Solemnly.*) Cyrano, assume the Bergerac accent once more!

DE GUICHE (*looking at the house*). Yes, it is there. I don't see well. This mask hinders me! (*He starts to go in; Cyrano jumps from the balcony, holding on to the branch, which bends and lets him down between the door and De Guiche; he pretends to fall heavily, as if from a considerable height, and lies flat on the ground, where he remains motionless, as if stunned. De Guiche jumps back.*) What? What is this? (*When he raises his eyes the branch has sprung back; he sees nothing but the sky and cannot understand it.*) Where did this man fall from?

CYRANO (*sitting up and with the Gascony accent*). From the moon!

DE GUICHE. From the what?

CYRANO (*in a sleepy voice*). What time is it?

DE GUICHE. Has he lost his reason?

CYRANO. What time is it? What country? What day? What season?

DE GUICHE. But—

CYRANO. I am bewildered!

DE GUICHE. Sir—

CYRANO. I fell like a bomb from the moon!

DE GUICHE (*out of patience*). Ah! come now, sir!

CYRANO (*rising, in a terrible voice*). I fell from it!

DE GUICHE (*drawing back*). Well! let it be so! You fell from it! Perhaps he is demented!

CYRANO (*stepping toward him*). And I didn't fall metaphorically!

DE GUICHE. But—

CYRANO. A hundred years, or perhaps one minute ago.—I have no idea how long my fall lasted!—I was in that saffron-colored orb!

DE GUICHE (*shrugging his shoulders*). Yes. Let me pass!

CYRANO (*getting in his way*). Where am I? Be frank with me! Disguise nothing! In what place, on what site, have I just fallen, sir, like an aerolite?

DE GUICHE. Zounds!

CYRANO. While falling I could make no choice about my destination,—and I do not know where I fell!—Is it in a moon or on an earth that the weight of my posterior has brought me?

DE GUICHE. But I tell you, sir—

CYRANO (*with a cry of terror which makes De Guiche draw back*). Ha! Good Lord! I believe the people I see in this country have black faces!

DE GUICHE (*bringing his hand to his face*). What?

CYRANO (*with decided fear*). Am I in Algeria? Are you a native?

DE GUICHE (*having felt his mask*). This mask!

CYRANO (*pretending to be somewhat reassured*). Then I am in Venice, or in Genoa?

DE GUICHE (*trying to pass by*). A lady is waiting for me!

CYRANO (*completely reassured*). Then I am in Paris.

DE GUICHE (*smiling in spite of himself*). The fellow is droll enough!

CYRANO. Ah! you are laughing?

DE GUICHE. I am laughing, but I wish to pass!

CYRANO (*beaming*). I have fallen in Paris! (*Perfectly at his ease, laughing, brushing himself, bowing.*) I have arrived—excuse me—by the last cloud-burst. I am somewhat covered with ether. I have had a journey of it! My eyes are filled with star dust. I still have some planet fur on my spurs! (*Picking something off his sleeve.*) Wait, here is a comet's hair on my doublet!

(*He pretends to blow it away.*)

DE GUICHE (*beside himself*). Sir!

CYRANO (*just as he is going to pass, stretches out his leg as if to show him something on it, and stops him*). I have brought a tooth from the Great Bear in the calf of my leg—and as I brushed past the Trident, in trying to avoid one of the prongs, I sat down in the scales, the indicator of which up there now marks my weight! (*Quickly preventing De Guiche from passing and taking him by a button on his doublet.*) If you should press my nose, sir, between your fingers, milk would spurt out from it!

DE GUICHE. What? Milk?

CYRANO. From the Milky Way!

DE GUICHE. Oh! By the infernal regions!

CYRANO. It was Heaven that despatched me! (*Folding his arms.*) No! Would you believe it, I saw just now, as I fell, that Sirius wraps his head in a turban at night? (*Confidentially.*) The other Bear is too small as yet to bite. (*Laughing.*) I broke a string as I passed through the Lyre! (*Proudly.*) But I count on writing a book about all this, and the golden stars which I have just brought with me, in my singed cloak, at great danger and risk, will serve as asterisks when it is printed!

DE GUICHE. Now at last, I wish—

CYRANO. I see what you are coming to!

DE GUICHE. Sir!

CYRANO. You would like to learn from my lips how the moon is made and if any one dwells in the rotundity of this cucurbit?

DE GUICHE (*shouting*). No! I wish—

CYRANO. To know how I mounted there? It was by a means of my own invention.

DE GUICHE (*discouraged*). He is mad!

CYRANO (*scornfully*). I did not repeat the stupid eagle of Regiomontanus, nor the timid pigeon of Archytas!

DE GUICHE. He is a lunatic,—but he is a learned lunatic.

CYRANO. No, I did not imitate anything which had been done before! (*De Guiche succeeds in passing by and walks toward Roxane's door; Cyrano follows him, ready to seize him.*) I invented six ways of violating the virgin azure!

DE GUICHE. Six?

CYRANO (*with volubility*). I could caparison my body, made bare as a wax taper, with crystal phials filled full of tears from a morning sky, and my person then exposed to the rays of the sun would be sucked up by that luminary, in sucking up the dew!

DE GUICHE (*surprised and taking a step toward Cyrano*). Wait! Yes, that makes one!

CYRANO (*drawing back to lead him on the other side*). And again I could imprison enough wind to take my flight, by rarefying the air in a cedar chest by means of glowing mirrors on an icosahedron!

DE GUICHE (*takes another step*). Two!

CYRANO (*again drawing back*). Or else, since I am a machinist as well as pyrotechnist, on a "grasshopper" with steel springs, by successive explosions of saltpetre, hurl myself into the blue meadows where the stars are feeding!

DE GUICHE (*following him, without a suspicion, and counting on his fingers*). Three!

CYRANO. Since smoke has a tendency to rise, blow enough into a globe to carry me away!

DE GUICHE (*same action, more and more astonished*). Four!

CYRANO. Since Diana, when her bow is slenderest, loves to suck out, O oxen, your marrow—to anoint myself with it!

DE GUICHE (*stupefied*). Five.

CYRANO (*who while talking has led him to the other side of the square, near a seat*). Finally, placing myself on an iron plate, take a piece of loadstone and fling it in the air! This is an excellent way: the iron rushes off in pursuit, as soon as the loadstone starts away; you hurl the loadstone very quickly again, and, zounds! you can ascend in this way indefinitely.

DE GUICHE. Six! Those are six excellent ways! Which method of the six, did you choose, sir?

CYRANO. A seventh!

DE GUICHE. Indeed! What was that?

CYRANO. I give you a hundred guesses!

DE GUICHE. The rascal is growing interesting!

CYRANO (*making the sound of waves with grand, mysterious gestures*). Houle! houle!

DE GUICHE. Well?

CYRANO. Have you guessed?

DE GUICHE. No!

CYRANO. The sea! Just at the time the tide is attracted by the moon I take my place on the sand—after a sea-bath— and head first, my dear,—for the hair especially holds the water in its fringe!—I rise in the air, straight, straight up, like an angel. I ascend, I ascend gently, without effort, when I feel a shock!—Then—

DE GUICHE (*carried away by curiosity and sitting down on the seat*). Then?

CYRANO. Then— (*Resuming his natural voice.*) The quarter of an hour is past, sir,—I give you up: the marriage is over.

DE GUICHE (*leaping to his feet*). What is this? I am drunk! That voice? (*The door of the house opens. Lackeys appear carrying lighted candelabras. Light. Cyrano takes off his hat with the brim turned down*). And that nose! Cyrano?

CYRANO (*bowing*). Cyrano. They have just this moment exchanged rings.

DE GUICHE. Who? (*He turns around. Tableau. Behind the Lackeys, Roxane and Christian holding hands. The Capuchin follows them smiling. Ragueneau also carries a torch. The Duenna brings up the rear, flurried, in a wrapper.*) Heavens!

SCENE TWELFTH

The Same, ROXANE, CHRISTIAN, *the* Capuchin, RAGUENEAU, Lackeys, *the* Duenna

DE GUICHE (*to Roxane*). You! (*Stupefied at recognizing Christian.*) To him? (*Bowing to Roxane with admiration.*) You are one of the shrewdest! (*To Cyrano.*) My compliments, Mr. Machine-inventor: your tale would have stopped a saint at the gate of Paradise! Make a note of the details, because it really is worth preserving in a book!

CYRANO (*bowing*). Sir, that is advice I promise to follow.

THE CAPUCHIN (*pointing out the lovers to De Guiche and*

shaking his great white beard with satisfaction). A handsome couple, my son, united by you!

DE GUICHE (*giving him a freezing look*). Yes. (*To Roxane.*) Will you say farewell, madame, to your husband?

ROXANE. What?

DE GUICHE (*to Christian*). The regiment is already on the way. Join it!

ROXANE. To go to war?

DE GUICHE. Certainly.

ROXANE. But, sir, the cadets are not going!

DE GUICHE. They will go. (*Taking out the paper which he had put into his pocket.*) Here is the order. (*To Christian.*) Run and carry it, baron.

ROXANE (*throwing herself into Christian's arms*). Christian!

DE GUICHE (*sneeringly, to Cyrano*). The wedding-night is still remote!

CYRANO (*aside*). He thinks he is causing me enormous pain.

CHRISTIAN (*to Roxane*). Oh! your lips once more!

CYRANO. Come, come; enough!

CHRISTIAN (*continuing to kiss Roxane*). It is hard to leave her. You do not know.

CYRANO (*trying to get him away*). I know.

(*In the distance drums are heard beating a march.*)

DE GUICHE (*going to the back of the stage*). The regiment is leaving.

ROXANE (*to Cyrano, detaining Christian, whom he is still trying to take away*). Oh! I intrust him to your care! Promise me that nothing shall endanger his life!

CYRANO. I will try—but still I cannot promise . . .

ROXANE (*same action*). Promise that he will be very cautious!

CYRANO. Yes, I will try, but . . .

ROXANE (*same action*). That he will never be cold in this terrible siege!

CYRANO. I will do my best, but . . .

ROXANE (*same action*). That he will be faithful!

CYRANO. Oh! Yes! Certainly, but . . .

ROXANE (*same action*). That he will write me often!
CYRANO (*stopping*). That, I promise you!

(*Curtain falls.*)

ACT FOURTH

The Gascon Cadets

The post occupied by the company of CARBON DE CASTEL-JALOUX *at the siege of Arras. In the background, a talus crossing the whole stage. Beyond is a view of a plain: the country is covered with earthworks. The walls of Arras and the silhouette of its roofs against the sky, in the distance. Tents, scattered arms, drums, etc. Daylight is just dawning. The east is yellow. Sentinels at regular intervals. Fires. The Gascon Cadets, wrapped in their cloaks, are sleeping.* CARBON DE CASTEL-JALOUX *and* LE BRET *are on the watch. They are very pale and thin.* CHRISTIAN *is asleep among the others, in his cape, in the foreground, his face lighted up by a fire. Silence.*

SCENE FIRST

CHRISTIAN, CARBON DE CASTEL-JALOUX, LE BRET, *the* Cadets,
then CYRANO

LE BRET. It is frightful!

CARBON. Yes.

LE BRET. Nothing less. 'Sdeath!

CARBON (*motioning to him to speak lower*). Whisper your
swearing! You will wake them up. (*To the Cadets.*) Hush!
Sleep! (*To Le Bret.*) He who sleeps, is dining! When one has
insomnia, he finds out how little he has! What a famine!

(*Firing is heard in the distance.*)

CARBON. Ah! Curse that firing! They will wake up my boys!
(*To the Cadets, who lift up their heads.*) Sleep!

(*They lie down again. Renewed firing nearer.*)

A CADET (*moving*). The deuce! Again?

CARBON. It is nothing! It is Cyrano coming back!

(*The heads which were raised fall back again.*)

A SENTINEL (*outside*). Odds-bodikins! Who goes there?

CYRANO'S VOICE. Bergerac!

THE SENTINEL (*on the talus*). Odds-bodikins! Who goes
there?

CYRANO (*appearing on the rampart*). Bergerac, fool!

(*He comes forward.* LE BRET, *anxious, goes to meet him.*)

LE BRET. Ah! Good God!

CYRANO (*motioning to him not to waken any one*). Hush!

LE BRET. Wounded?

CYRANO. You know very well that they have a habit of miss-
ing me every morning!

LE BRET. It is rather rough to risk your life to carry a letter
every day at dawn!

CYRANO (*stopping in front of Christian*). I promised that
he should write often! (*He looks at him.*) He is asleep. He is
pale. If the poor little girl knew how he is dying of hunger—
But always handsome!

LE BRET. Go quickly and get some sleep!

CYRANO. Don't growl, Le Bret! Know this: that in order to
pass through the Spanish ranks, I have chosen a place where
they are drunk every night.

LE BRET. You ought, some day, to bring us back some food.

CYRANO. I must be light to pass through!— But I know that
there will be news to-night. The French will eat or die,—if I
have seen aright.

LE BRET. Tell me about it!

CYRANO. No. I am not sure— You will see!

CARBON. What a shame when besieging to be famished!

LE BRET. Alas! Nothing is more complicated than this siege
of Arras. We are besieging Arras,—we ourselves, taken in a
trap, are besieged by the Cardinal Infanto of Spain.

CYRANO. Some one ought to come and besiege him in his
turn.

LE BRET. I cannot laugh.

CYRANO. Oh! ho!

LE BRET. To think that every day you risk a life like yours,
you wretch, to carry— (*Seeing him go toward one of the
tents.*) Where are you going?

CYRANO. I am going to write another.

(*He lifts the canvas and disappears.*)

SCENE SECOND

The Same, without CYRANO

(*The daylight is increasing. Rosy light in the sky. The town
of Arras is gilded on the horizon. A cannon is heard, immedi-*

ately followed by the beating of drums, in the far distance toward the left. Other drums beat nearer. The drum beats answer one another and, coming together, almost burst forth on the stage and die away toward the right, running through the camp. The reveille. Sounds of awakening. Distant voices of officers.)

CARBON (*with a sigh*). The reveille!—Alas! (*The Cadets stir in their cloaks, and stretch themselves.*) Succulent sleep, thou comest to an end! I know too well what their first cry will be!

A CADET (*sitting up*). I am hungry!

ANOTHER. I am dying!

ALL. Oh!

CARBON. Get up!

THIRD CADET. Not another step!

FOURTH CADET. Not another motion!

THE FIRST (*looking at himself in his cuirass*). My tongue is yellow: the weather is indigestible!

ANOTHER. My baron's torse for a little Chester!

ANOTHER. If no one will furnish my stomach with something to elaborate a pint of chyle for me, I shall retire to my tent—like Achilles!

ANOTHER. Yes, some bread!

CARBON (*going to the tent where Cyrano is, in a low voice*). Cyrano!

OTHERS. We are dying!

CARBON (*still speaking low at the door of the tent*). Help me! You who always have a merry answer for them, come and cheer them up!

SECOND CADET (*rushing toward the first, who is chewing something*). What are you nibbling?

THE FIRST. Gun-wadding, they were frying in helmets in axle-grease. The region around Arras has very little game!

ANOTHER (*entering*). I have just been hunting!

ANOTHER (*entering*). I have been fishing in the Scarpe!

ALL (*getting up, rush at the two just come in*). What? What did you bring back? A pheasant? A carp? Quick, quick, show us!

THE FISHERMAN. A gudgeon!

THE HUNTER. A sparrow!

ALL (*exasperated*). Enough! Let us revolt!

CARBON. Help us, Cyrano.

(*It is now broad daylight.*)

SCENE THIRD

The Same, CYRANO

CYRANO (*coming out of his tent, calm, with a pen behind his ear, a book in his hand*). What is it? (*Silence. To the First Cadet.*) Why do you walk with such a dragging gait?

THE CADET. I have something in my heels which impedes me.

CYRANO. What is it?

THE CADET. My stomach!

CYRANO. I have the same difficulty, truly!

THE CADET. It must impede you?

CYRANO. No, it helps me along.

SECOND CADET. My teeth are long!

CYRANO. You will take all the larger mouthfuls.

A THIRD. My belly sounds hollow!

CYRANO. We will beat the charge on it.

ANOTHER. I have a buzzing in my ears.

CYRANO. No, no; famished belly, not ears; you lie!

ANOTHER. Oh! for something to eat,—with oil!

CYRANO (*taking off his helmet and putting it in his hand*). Your sallet.

ANOTHER. What is there I can devour?

CYRANO (*throwing him the book he is holding*). The "Iliad."

ANOTHER. The minister, in Paris, has his four meals.

CYRANO. Do you think he ought to send you a young partridge?

THE SAME. Why not? And some wine!

CYRANO. Richelieu, Burgundy, if you please?

THE SAME. By some Capuchin!

CYRANO. His intoxicating eminence?

ANOTHER. I am as hungry as an ogre!

CYRANO. Well! You are eating the bread of dependency.

THE FIRST CADET (*shrugging his shoulders*). Always witty, always to the point.

CYRANO. Yes, the point, wit! I should like to die some night, under a rosy sky, making a witty remark for a fine cause! Oh! struck by the only noble weapon, and by a worthy enemy on the glorious turf far from a bed of sickness, to fall with the sword-point in my heart and a pointed speech on my lips!

ALL (*exclaim*). I am hungry.

CYRANO (*folding his arms*). Indeed! Do you think of nothing but eating? Draw near, Bertrandou the fifer, once a shepherd; from your double leather case draw out one of your pipes, blow and play to this set of gormandizers and gluttons, those old airs of our country, with their sweet captivating rhythm, each note of which is like a little sister, and in which remain captive the sounds of loved voices, those airs whose slow motion is like the smoke our native hamlet breathes forth from its roofs, those airs the music of which seems to be a patois! (*The old man sits down and gets his fife ready.*) Let the warlike flute, which mourns to-day, for a moment, while your fingers seem to dance a bird minuet on its stops, recollect that before it was ebony it was a reed; let its song surprise it, let it recognize the soul of its rustic and peaceful youth! (*The old man begins to play some Languedocian airs.*) Listen, Gascons! Under his fingers it is no longer the shrill fife of the camp, it is the flute of the woods! It is no longer the call to combat, it is the slow galoubet of our goatherds! Listen! It is the vale, the moor, the forest, the little brown shepherd in his red cap, it is the tender green of evening on the Dordogne—listen, Gascons: it is all Gascony!

(*Every head is bent; every eye dreamy;—and tears are furtively wiped away, with the back of a sleeve or the corner of a cloak.*)

CARBON (*to Cyrano, in a low voice*). But you are making them weep!

CYRANO. From homesickness! A nobler pain than hunger! not physical: spiritual! I like to have their suffering changed from their vitals, and let it be their hearts now that ache!

CARBON. You will weaken them by moving them to tears!

CYRANO (*having motioned to the drummer to approach*). Nonsense! The heroism in their blood is quickly aroused! It is only necessary—

(*He makes a sign. The drum rolls.*)

ALL (*rising, and rushing for their arms*). What? What? What is it?

CYRANO (*smiling*). You see, the rolling of the drum was enough! Farewell dreams, regrets, the old province, love— what the piper aroused, the drum puts to flight!

A CADET (*looking toward the back of the stage*). Ah! Ah! Here is Monsieur de Guiche!

ALL THE CADETS (*murmuring*). Hou—

CYRANO (*smiling*). A murmur of flattery!

A CADET. He bores us!

ANOTHER. With his wide lace collar over his armor, he carries his head high!

ANOTHER. As if one wore linen over iron!

THE FIRST. It is a good thing when one has a boil on one's neck!

THE SECOND. Still a courtier!

ANOTHER. His uncle's nephew!

CARBON. Yet, he is a Gascon!

THE FIRST. A false one! Do not trust him! Because the Gascons—they must be mad: nothing is more dangerous than a reasonable Gascon.

LE BRET. He is pale!

ANOTHER. He is hungry—as much so as any poor devil! But as his cuirass is studded with silver-gilt, the cramp in his stomach sparkles in the sun!

CYRANO (*quickly*). Don't show that you are suffering! Bring out your cards, your pipes, and your dice— (*all quickly begin to play on their drums, their stools, on the ground, and on their cloaks; they light long tobacco pipes*)—and I will read Descartes.

(*He walks back and forth, reading in a little book he has taken out of his pocket. Tableau.* DE GUICHE *enters. Everybody looks absorbed and happy. He is very pale. He goes toward* CARBON.)

SCENE FOURTH

The Same, DE GUICHE

DE GUICHE (*to Carbon*). Ah!—Good morning! (*They look at each other, aside, with satisfaction.*) He is green.

CARBON (*same action*). He is all eyes.

DE GUICHE (*looking at the Cadets*). So here are those quarrelsome fellows? Yes, gentlemen, it comes to me from all sides that I am jeered at, that the cadets, the nobility of the mountains, country squires of Béarn, barons of Périgord, cannot be scornful enough of their colonel, call me intriguing, a courtier, —that it disturbs them to see a point-lace collar over my cuirass —and that they are continually indignant because one can be a Gascon without being a beggar! (*Silence. They go on playing and smoking.*) Shall I have you punished by your captain? No.

CARBON. Moreover, I am free and inflict no punishments.

DE GUICHE. Ah?

CARBON. I have paid my company. It is mine. I only obey orders of war.

DE GUICHE. Ah? My faith! That is enough. (*Addressing the Cadets.*) I scorn your bravadoes. My way of standing fire is well known; yesterday at Bapaume the fury with which I forced the Count de Bucquoi to yield was seen: pouring my men on his, like an avalanche, I charged three times!

CYRANO (*without looking up from his book*). And your white scarf?

DE GUICHE (*surprised and satisfied*). You know that detail? Indeed, it happened that while I was wheeling about to collect my men for the third charge, a crowd of fugitives dragged me to the edge of the enemy's lines; I was in danger of being taken and shot, when I had the good sense to untie and drop the scarf which announced my military rank; so, without attracting attention, I was able to leave the Spanish and coming back, with all my men revived, to beat them!—Well, what do you say to this feat?

(*The* Cadets *do not appear to be listening; but here the cards and dice boxes remain suspended, the smoke from their pipes stays in their cheeks: pause.*)

CYRANO. That Henry Fourth would never have consented, when overpowered by numbers, to relinquish his white plume.

(*Silent joy. The cards are laid down. The dice fall. The smoke escapes.*)

DE GUICHE. The trick succeeded, however!

(*The same pause suspending the games and pipes.*)

CYRANO. It is possible, but one does not renounce the honor of being a target. (*Cards are laid down, dice fall, smoke escapes with increasing satisfaction.*) If I had been present when the scarf dropped,—my courage, sir, differs from yours in this respect,—I should have picked it up and put it on.

DE GUICHE. Yes, your Gascon boastfulness, again.

CYRANO. Boastfulness? Lend it to me. I offer to lead the attack to-night, wearing it over my shoulder.

DE GUICHE. Again the offer of a Gascon! You know that the scarf is with the enemy, on the borders of the Scarpe, in a place riddled with grape-shot, where no one can go to find it!

CYRANO (*taking the white scarf out of his pocket, and handing it to him*). There it is.

(*Silence. The* Cadets *smother their laughter in their cards and their dice boxes.* DE GUICHE *turns around and looks at them: they immediately recover their gravity, and continue their games; one of them whistles indifferently the mountain air played by the piper.*)

DE GUICHE (*taking the scarf*). Thank you. With this light piece of stuff I can make a signal,—which I was hesitating to do.

(*He goes to the talus, climbs up on it, and waves the scarf in the air several times.*)

ALL. What?

THE SENTINEL (*on the top of the talus*). A man down there is running away!

DE GUICHE (*coming down*). He is a false Spanish spy. He renders us great service. The information he carries to the enemy is what I give him, so that we can influence their decisions.

CYRANO. He is a scamp.

(*Tying a knot in his scarf with indifference.*)

DE GUICHE. It is very convenient. We were saying— Oh! I was going to tell you a fact. This very night, making one last effort to get food for us, the marshal went to Dourlens, without drums; the King's sutlers are there; he will join them through the fields; but to come back without hindrance, he has taken such a number of troops that there is a fine opportunity to attack us: half of the army is absent from the camp!

CARBON. Yes, if the Spanish knew it, it would be grave. But they are not aware of their absence?

DE GUICHE. They know it. They are going to attack us.

CARBON. Ah!

DE GUICHE. My false spy has come to warn me of their approach. He said: "I can determine the place; at what point would you like to have them make the attack? I shall say where it is the least defended, and the attempt will be made there." I replied: "That is good. Leave the camp. Follow the line with your eyes, it will be at the point where I signal to you."

CARBON (*to the Cadets*). Gentlemen, get ready.

(*All rise. Sound of buckling on swords and belts.*)

DE GUICHE. It will be in an hour.

FIRST CADET. Ah! Well.

(*They all sit down again, and go on with what they were doing.*)

DE GUICHE (*to Carbon*). You must gain time. The marshal is coming back.

CARBON. And in order to gain time?

DE GUICHE. You will be so obliging as to give your lives.

CYRANO. Ah! Is that your vengeance?

DE GUICHE. I shall not pretend that if I loved you I should have chosen you and yours, but, as no one can compare to you in boastfulness, I serve my King in serving my spite.

CYRANO. Allow me to express my gratitude to you, sir.

DE GUICHE. I know that you love to fight alone against a hundred: you will not complain of lacking the opportunity.

(*He goes back with* CARBON.)

CYRANO (*to the Cadets*). Well, then, we shall add to the Gascon coat-of-arms, which bears six chevrons, gentlemen, azure and or, a chevron of blood, which it lacks as yet!

(DE GUICHE *talks low with* CARBON DE CASTEL-JALOUX, *at the back of the stage. They give orders. They prepare for the defence.* CYRANO *goes toward* CHRISTIAN, *who remains motionless, with folded arms.*)

CYRANO (*putting his hand on his shoulder*). Christian?

CHRISTIAN (*shaking his head*). Roxane!

CYRANO. Alas!

CHRISTIAN. At least, I wish I could put all my heart's farewell into a beautiful letter!

CYRANO. I suspected that it would be for to-day. (*He takes a note out of his doublet*). So I have written your farewell.

CHRISTIAN. Let me see it!

CYRANO. Do you wish it?

CHRISTIAN (*taking the letter*). Why, yes! (*He opens it, reads, and stops.*) Wait!

CYRANO. What is it?

CHRISTIAN. This little spot?

CYRANO (*taking the letter quickly, and looking at it innocently*). A spot?

CHRISTIAN. It is a tear!

CYRANO. Yes. A poet gets carried away by his theme, that is the charm of it! You understand—this note—was very touching: it made me weep myself to write it.

CHRISTIAN. Weep?

CYRANO. Yes—because—to die is not terrible. But—never to see her again—that is horrible! For I should—(*Christian looks at him*) we should—(*quickly*) you would—

CHRISTIAN (*snatching the letter from him*). Give me that note!

(*A distant noise is heard in the camp.*)

A SENTINEL'S VOICE. Odds-bodikins, who goes there?

(*Firing. Sounds of voices. Bells.*)

CARBON. What is it?

THE SENTINEL (*on the talus*). A coach!

(*They rush to see.*)

EXCLAMATIONS. What! In the camp?—It is coming in!—It seems to come from the enemy!—The deuce! Fire!—No, the coachman has cried out!—Cried out what?—He has cried out: Service of the King!

(*Everybody is on the talus, watching. The bells draw near.*)

DE GUICHE. What? Of the King!

(*They come down and fall into line.*)

CARBON. Hats off, all of you!

DE GUICHE (*from behind the scenes.*) The King! Clear the way, vile rabble, that it may have room to draw up in style!

(*The coach enters on the full trot. It is covered with mud and dust. The curtains are drawn. Two lackeys behind. It stops short.*)

CARBON (*shouting*). Beat a salute!
(*The drums roll. All the* Cadets *uncover.*)
DE GUICHE. Lower the steps!
(*Two men hasten to the coach. The door opens.*)
ROXANE (*jumping out of the coach*). Good morning!

(*The sound of a woman's voice makes all these people, who are reverently bowing their heads, suddenly look up. Amazement.*)

SCENE FIFTH

The Same, ROXANE

DE GUICHE. Service of the King! You?
ROXANE. Of the only king, Love!
CYRANO. Ah! Great God!
CHRISTIAN (*darting toward her*). You! Why have you come?
ROXANE. The siege was too long!
CHRISTIAN. Why?
ROXANE. I will tell you!
CYRANO (*who, at the sound of her voice, stood nailed to the spot, motionless, without daring to turn his eyes toward her*). My God! shall I look at her?
DE GUICHE. You cannot stay here!
ROXANE (*gayly*). Oh, yes! yes! Will you bring me a drum? (*She sits down on a drum, which is brought to her.*) There, thank you! (*She laughs.*) They fired on my coach! (*Proudly.*) A patrol! It looks as if it were made out of a pumpkin, doesn't it? as in the fairy-tale, and the lackeys out of rats. (*Throwing a kiss to Christian.*) Good morning! (*Looking at them all.*) You don't look gay! Do you know how far it is to Arras? (*Noticing Cyrano.*) Cousin, I am charmed!
CYRANO (*approaching*). Ah, indeed! How?—
ROXANE. How did I find the army? Oh! dear me, my friend, it was very easy: I followed where I saw the country laid

waste. Oh! I had to see these horrors to believe them! Gentlemen, if this is the service of your King, mine is better!

CYRANO. This is madness! Where the devil could you have passed through?

ROXANE. Where? Through the Spanish lines.

FIRST CADET. Ah! They are ugly fellows!

DE GUICHE. How did you manage to cross their lines?

LE BRET. That must have been very difficult?

ROXANE. Not very. I simply drove through as fast as possible If some hidalgo showed his haughty face I put on my sweetest smile at the door, and as these gentlemen—no disparagement to the French—are the most gallant in the world, I was able to pass.

CARBON. Yes, surely, that smile of yours is a passport. But they must have called upon you frequently to tell them where you were going in this way, madame?

ROXANE. Frequently. Then I replied, "I am going to see my lover." Immediately the Spaniard, looking very fierce, would gravely close the carriage door, with a gesture the King would envy, motion away the muskets already pointed at me, and superb both in his grace and stateliness, with his spurs beneath his lace, straight as an organ pipe, sweeping the air with his plumed hat, would bow and say, "Pass on, señorita!"

CHRISTIAN. But Roxane—

ROXANE. I said, "my lover," yes—forgive me! You understand if I had said, "my husband," no one would have let me pass!

CHRISTIAN. But—

ROXANE. What is the matter with you?

DE GUICHE. You must go away from here!

ROXANE. I?

CYRANO. Very quickly!

LE BRET. As soon as possible!

CHRISTIAN. Yes.

ROXANE. But how?

CHRISTIAN (embarrassed). Because—

CYRANO (also embarrassed). In three-quarters of an hour—

DE GUICHE (*also embarrassed*). Or four—

CARBON (*also embarrassed*). It would be better—

LE BRET (*also embarrassed*). You could—

ROXANE. I shall remain. You are going to fight.

ALL. Oh! no!

ROXANE. He is my husband! (*She throws herself into Christian's arms.*) Let me be killed with you!

CHRISTIAN. What eyes you have!

ROXANE. I will tell you why!

DE GUICHE (*in despair*). It is a terrible position!

ROXANE (*turning around*). What! terrible?

CYRANO. And the proof of it is that he has given it to us!

ROXANE (*to De Guiche*). Ah! Do you wish me to be a widow?

DE GUICHE. Oh! I swear to you!

ROXANE. No! Now I am mad! And I am not going away! Besides, it is amusing.

CYRANO. What? Is the *précieuse* a heroine?

ROXANE. Monsieur de Bergerac. I am your cousin.

A CADET. We will defend you well!

ROXANE (*more and more excited*). I believe it, my friends!

ANOTHER (*carried away*). The whole camp smells of iris!

ROXANE. And I have put on a hat which will look very well in battle! (*Looking at De Guiche.*) But perhaps it is time for the Count to go away. They might begin.

DE GUICHE. Ah! this is too much! I am going to inspect my cannons and will return. You have still time to change your mind!

ROXANE. Never!

(DE GUICHE *goes out.*)

SCENE SIXTH

The Same, without DE GUICHE

CHRISTIAN (*imploringly*). Roxane!

ROXANE. No!

FIRST CADET (*to the others*). She is going to stay!

ALL (*rushing about, jostling each other, making themselves tidy*). A comb!—Soap!—My clothing is torn: a needle!—A ribbon!—Your mirror!—My ruffles!—Your mustache iron!—A razor!

ROXANE (*to Cyrano, who is still imploring her*). No! Nothing will make me stir from this place!

CARBON (*after tightening his buckles, dusting his clothes, like the others brushing his hat, arranging his plume, and drawing on his cuffs, goes toward Roxane, and ceremoniously*). Perhaps, if that is the case it would be proper for me to present to you some of these gentlemen who are going to have the honor of dying before your eyes.

(ROXANE *bows, and stands waiting, on* CHRISTIAN'S *arm.*)

CARBON (*presents*). Baron de Peyrescous de Colignac!

THE CADET (*bowing*). Madame—

CARBON (*continuing*). Baron de Casterac de Cahuzac.— Vidame de Malgouyre Estressac Lésbas d'Escarabiot.—Chevalier d'Antignac-Juzet.—Baron Hillot de Blagnac-Saléchan de Castel Crabioules . . .

ROXANE. How many names have you apiece?

BARON HILLOT. Multitudes!

CARBON (*to Roxane*). Open the hand which holds your handkerchief.

ROXANE (*opens her hand and the handkerchief drops*). Why? (*The whole company starts as if to rush forward and pick it up.*)

CARBON (*quickly picking it up*). My company was without a flag! But by my faith the handsomest in the camp is going to float above it!

ROXANE (*smiling*). It is rather small.

CARBON (*fastening the handkerchief to the handle of his captain's lance*). But it is of lace!

A CADET (*to the others*). I should die without a regret after seeing this pretty face, had I but a single nut in my belly!

CARBON (*hearing him, with indignation*). Fie! To speak of eating when an exquisite woman—

ROXANE. But the air of the camp is keen, and I myself am famished: patties, cold meats, fine wine—that is my bill of fare! Will you bring me all that?

A CADET. All that!

ANOTHER. Good Lord, where should we get it?

ROXANE (*calmly*). From my carriage.

ALL. What?

ROXANE. But you will have to serve and carve and bone it! Look at my coachman a little closer, gentlemen, and you will recognize a valuable man: every sauce shall be served hot if you like!

THE CADETS (*rushing toward the carriage*). It is Ragueneau! (*Cheers.*) Oh! Oh!

ROXANE (*watching them*). Poor fellows!

CYRANO (*kissing her hand*). Good fairy!

RAGUENEAU (*standing on the seat like a charlatan in a public square*). Gentlemen!

(*Enthusiasm.*)

THE CADETS. Bravo! Bravo!

RAGUENEAU. The Spanish did not see the feast, when they let such charm pass by!

(*Applause.*)

CYRANO (*in a low voice to Christian*). Hum! hum! Christian!

RAGUENEAU. Carried away by gallantry, they did not see— (*he takes from under his seat a dish, which he holds up*)— the fowl!

(*Applause: The fowl is passed from one to another.*)

CYRANO (*in a low voice to Christian*). I beg you, just one word!

RAGUENEAU. And Venus knew how to hold their eyes, while Diana secretly passed—(*brandishing a leg of mutton*)—her venison!

(*Enthusiasm. The leg of mutton seized by twenty outstretched hands.*)

CYRANO (*in a low voice to Christian*). I should like to speak to you!

ROXANE (*to the Cadets, who are coming back with their arms filled with food*). Lay that on the ground!

(*She lays a cloth on the grass, assisted by two imperturbable lackeys who were behind the coach.*)

ROXANE (*to Christian, just as Cyrano was going to take him aside*). Make yourself useful!

(CHRISTIAN *comes to her assistance.* CYRANO *appears impatient.*)

RAGUENEAU. A truffled peacock!

FIRST CADET (*beaming as he comes forward cutting off a large slice of ham*). Thunder! We shall not have to run our last chance without having a final feed. (*Quickly recollecting himself when he sees Roxane.*) I beg your pardon! a royal feast!

RAGUENEAU (*throwing the cushions out of the coach*). The cushions are filled with ortolans!

(*Uproar. They rip open the cushions. Laughter. Delight.*)

THIRD CADET. Ah! Landlord!

RAGUENEAU (*throwing out bottles of red wine*). Flasks of ruby! (*White wine.*) Flasks of topaz!

ROXANE (*throwing a folded tablecloth in Cyrano's face*). Unfold that tablecloth! Ah! Come, be lively!

RAGUENEAU (*waving one of the lanterns he has pulled off*). Each lantern is a little larder!

CYRANO (*in a low voice to Christian, while they are arranging the cloth together*). I must speak to you before you speak to her!

RAGUENEAU (*growing more and more poetical*). My whip-handle is a huge sausage!

ROXANE (*pouring out some wine and serving it*). Since they are going to kill us, zounds, let us laugh at the rest of the army! Yes, everything for the Gascons! And if De Guiche comes, he comes uninvited! (*Going from one to another.*) There, you have time enough. Do not eat so fast! Drink a little. Why do you weep?

FIRST CADET. It is too good!

ROXANE. Hush! Red or white? Some bread for Monsieur de Carbon! A knife! Your plate! A little crust? Some more? I will serve you! Some champagne? A wing?

CYRANO (*who follows her, his arms loaded with dishes, helping to serve*). I adore her.

ROXANE (*going toward Christian*). What will you have?

CHRISTIAN. Nothing.

ROXANE. Yes, this biscuit, in some muscat—just two fingers!

CHRISTIAN (*trying to detain her*). Oh! tell me why you came.

ROXANE. I must attend to these unfortunate fellows now. Hush! By and by—

LE BRET (*who has gone to the back of the stage, to pass some bread on the point of a lance to the sentinel on the talus*). De Guiche!

CYRANO. Quick! hide the bottles, dishes, pots, and hampers! Show nothing in your faces! (*To Ragueneau.*) Leap up to your seat! Is everything hidden?

(*In a twinkling everything is pushed into the tents or hidden under their clothing, under their cloaks, in hats.* DE GUICHE *enters in haste and stops suddenly, sniffing the air. Silence.*)

SCENE SEVENTH

The Same, DE GUICHE

DE GUICHE. It smells good.

A CADET (*humming a snatch of a tune*). To lo lo!

DE GUICHE (*stopping and looking at him*). What is the matter with you? You are very red!

THE CADET. Me? Nothing. It is my blood. We are going to have a battle; it stirs within me!

ANOTHER. Pum—pum—pum.

DE GUICHE (*turning around*). What is that?

THE CADET (*slightly intoxicated*). Nothing! It is a song! A little—

DE GUICHE. You are gay, my boy!

THE CADET. The approach of danger!

DE GUICHE (*calling to Carbon de Castel-Jaloux, to give an order*). Captain! I— (*He stops when he sees him.*) The deuce! You look good-natured, too!

CARBON (*turning crimson, and hiding a bottle behind his back with an evasive gesture*). Oh!

DE GUICHE. There is one cannon left, which I have had brought—(*he points to a place in the wing*)—there, in that corner, and your men can use it, if necessary.

A CADET (*swaggering*). Charming attention!

ANOTHER (*smiling graciously*). Sweet solicitude!

DE GUICHE. Ah! They are mad! (*Dryly.*) As you are quite unused to cannon, look out for the recoil.

THE FIRST CADET. Ah! Pft!

DE GUICHE (*furious, going toward him*). But!

THE CADET. The Gascon's cannon never recoils!

DE GUICHE (*taking him by the arm and shaking him*). You are drunk! What have you had?

THE CADET (*haughtily*). The smell of gun-powder!

DE GUICHE (*shrugging his shoulders, pushes him away and goes quickly to Roxane*). Quick, will you deign to give your decision, madame?

ROXANE. I shall remain.

DE GUICHE. Escape!

ROXANE. No!

DE GUICHE. Since it must be so, give me a musket!

CARBON. What?

DE GUICHE. I shall remain too.

CYRANO. At last, sir, you show pure bravery!

FIRST CADET. Can it be that you are a Gascon, in spite of your lace?

ROXANE. What!

DE GUICHE. I never leave a woman in danger.

SECOND CADET (*to the First*). Say then! I think we might give him something to eat!

(*All the food reappears as if by magic.*)

DE GUICHE (*whose eyes brighten*). Food!

A THIRD CADET. It came out from under every jacket!

DE GUICHE (*controlling himself, haughtily*). Do you suppose that I will eat your remnants?

CYRANO (*bowing*). You are making progress!

DE GUICHE (*proudly*). I am going to fight, fasting.

FIRST CADET. He has the Gascon accent!

DE GUICHE (*laughing*). I?

THE CADET. He is one of us!

(*All begin to dance.*)

CARBON DE CASTEL-JALOUX (*having disappeared a moment before behind the talus, reappears on the rampart*). I have arranged my pikemen.

(*He points out a line of pikes showing above the talus.*)

DE GUICHE (*to Roxane, bowing*). Will you take my hand for the review?

(*She takes it; they go up on the talus. Every one uncovers and follows them.*)

CHRISTIAN (*going to Cyrano, hurriedly*). Speak quickly!

(*When* ROXANE *appears on the talus, the lances disappear from sight, lowered for salute; a shout is raised: she bows.*)

THE PIKEMEN (*outside*). Hurrah!

CHRISTIAN. What was your secret?

CYRANO. In case Roxane—

CHRISTIAN. Well?

CYRANO. Should speak to you about the letters?

CHRISTIAN. Yes, I know!

CYRANO. Don't be so stupid as to show surprise—

CHRISTIAN. At what?

CYRANO. I must tell you! Oh! dear me, it is quite simple, and I thought of it to-day when I saw her. You have—

CHRISTIAN. Speak quickly!

CYRANO. You have—have written oftener than you think.

CHRISTIAN. What?

CYRANO. Well, I took it upon me, I interpreted your passion! I wrote sometimes without telling you about it!

CHRISTIAN. Ah?

CYRANO. It is quite simple!

CHRISTIAN. But how did you manage it, when we are block-aded?

CYRANO. Oh! Before daylight I was able to cross—

CHRISTIAN (*folding his arms*). Ah! That was very simple also? And I wrote twice a week?—Three times?—Four?

CYRANO. More than that.

CHRISTIAN. Every day?

CYRANO. Yes, every day. Twice a day.

CHRISTIAN (*violently*). And that intoxicated you, and the intoxication was so great that you risked your life . . .

CYRANO (*seeing Roxane return*). Be silent! Not before her!

(*He goes back quickly to his tent.*)

153

SCENE EIGHTH

ROXANE, CHRISTIAN; Cadets, *coming and going at the back of the stage.* CARBON *and* DE GUICHE *give orders.*

ROXANE (*running to Christian*). Now, Christian!

CHRISTIAN (*taking her hands*). Now tell me why you came by these frightful roads through all these ranks of soldiers and reisters, to join me here?

ROXANE. It was on account of your letters!

CHRISTIAN. What do you say?

ROXANE. So much the worse for you if I have run these risks! Your letters intoxicated me! Ah! think how many you have written me in the last month, each one more beautiful than the last!

CHRISTIAN. What! for a few little love letters . . .

ROXANE. Be still! You cannot know! Heavens! I have adored thee, it is true, ever since that evening, when in a voice unfamiliar to me, under my window, your soul began to make itself known. Well! in your letters for the past month it seemed as if all the time I heard your voice, on that evening, so tender, enveloping you! So, much the worse for you, I hastened to you! Wise Penelope would not have stayed at home embroidering, if Ulysses had written as you have, but to join you, she would have been as mad as Helen, and sent her threads of wool flying!

CHRISTIAN. But . . .

ROXANE. I read them over and over again, I grew faint, I was thine. Each of those little leaves was like a petal flown from your soul. I felt at every word of those letters of flame, your love so powerful, so sincere . . .

CHRISTIAN. Ah! sincere and powerful? You felt it, Roxane?

ROXANE. Oh! how I felt it!

CHRISTIAN. And you have come?

ROXANE. I have come—(Oh, my Christian, my master! You

would lift me up if I should throw myself at your feet, but it is my soul that I lay there and you can never lift that up!)— I come to ask your pardon (and it is time to ask it, since death is threatening us!) for having insulted you at first, in my frivolity, by loving you for your beauty alone!

CHRISTIAN (*alarmed*). Ah! Roxane!

ROXANE. And later on, my dear, when I became less frivolous,—a bird which flutters about before flying entirely away,— your beauty held me, your soul carried me away, and I loved you for both together!

CHRISTIAN. And now?

ROXANE. Well, your better self, at last, has gained the victory over yourself, and it is only for your soul that I love you!

CHRISTIAN (*drawing back*). Ah! Roxane!

ROXANE. So be happy. For to be loved only for that which one is temporarily clothed in, ought to put an eager, noble heart to torture; but your dear mind blots out your face, and the beauty which at first attracted me, now that I see better,— I see no more!

CHRISTIAN. Oh!

ROXANE. Do you still have doubts of such a victory?

CHRISTIAN (*dolefully*). Roxane!

ROXANE. I understand, you cannot believe such love?

CHRISTIAN. I do not want such love! I want to be loved more simply for—

ROXANE. For what you have always been loved until now? Allow yourself to be loved in a better fashion!

CHRISTIAN. No! It was better before!

ROXANE. Ah! you don't understand anything about it. Now that I love you better, I love you truly! It is your real self, you understand, that I adore, and were you less brilliant—

CHRISTIAN. Say no more!

ROXANE. I should love you still! If all your beauty should suddenly vanish—

CHRISTIAN. Oh! Do not say that!

ROXANE. Yes! I do say it!

CHRISTIAN. What? If I were ugly?

ROXANE. If you were ugly! I swear it!

CHRISTIAN. My God!

ROXANE. Is your joy so deep?

CHRISTIAN (*in a choking voice*). Yes.

ROXANE. What is the matter?

CHRISTIAN (*gently pushing her away*). Nothing. I have something to say—wait a moment—

ROXANE. But?

CHRISTIAN (*pointing to a group of Cadets, at the back of stage*). My love is taking you from those poor fellows; go smile on them a little, since they are about to die—go!

ROXANE (*moved*). Dear Christian!

(*She goes toward the* Gascons, *who press respectfully around her.*)

SCENE NINTH

CHRISTIAN, CYRANO; *in the background* ROXANE *talking with* CARBON *and some* Cadets

CHRISTIAN (*calling toward Cyrano's tent*). Cyrano?

CYRANO (*appearing, armed for battle*). What is it? You look pale!

CHRISTIAN. She no longer loves me!

CYRANO. How can that be?

CHRISTIAN. You are the one she loves!

CYRANO. No!

CHRISTIAN. She only loves my soul!

CYRANO. No!

CHRISTIAN. Yes! It is really you whom she loves,—and you love her, too!

CYRANO. I?

CHRISTIAN. I know it.

CYRANO. It is true.

CHRISTIAN. You are madly in love with her.

CYRANO. More than that.

CHRISTIAN. Tell her so!

CYRANO. No!

CHRISTIAN. Why not?

CYRANO. Look at my face!

CHRISTIAN. She would love me if I were ugly.

CYRANO. She told you so?

CHRISTIAN. She did!

CYRANO. Ah! I am very glad she told you that! But go, go, do not believe anything so senseless! Heavens, I am glad she had the thought to express,—but go, do not take her at her word, go, do not become ugly; she would be too angry with me!

CHRISTIAN. That is what I wish to see!

CYRANO. No, no!

CHRISTIAN. Let her take her choice! Go and tell her all!

CYRANO. No, no! Do not torment me.

CHRISTIAN. Should I destroy your happiness because I am handsome? That is too unjust!

CYRANO. And should I bury yours because, thanks to the chance that gave us birth, I have the gift of expressing—what you perhaps feel?

CHRISTIAN. Tell her all!

CYRANO. He insists upon tempting me; it is too bad!

CHRISTIAN. I am tired of carrying about a rival within me!

CYRANO. Christian!

CHRISTIAN. Our clandestine union—without witnesses—can be broken, if we survive!

CYRANO. He persists!

CHRISTIAN. Yes, I wish to be loved for myself, or not at all! I am going to see what they are doing—wait! I am going to the other end of the post; I shall return: speak, and let her choose between us!

CYRANO. It will be you!

CHRISTIAN. Well—I hope so! (*He calls.*) Roxane!

CYRANO. No! No!

ROXANE (*hastening to him*). What is it?

CHRISTIAN. Cyrano has something important to tell you—

(*She goes quickly to* CYRANO. CHRISTIAN *goes out.*)

SCENE TENTH

ROXANE, CYRANO, *then* LE BRET, CARBON DE CASTEL-JALOUX, *the* Cadets, RAGUENEAU, DE GUICHE, *etc.*

ROXANE. Important?

CYRANO (*distracted*). He is going! (*To Roxane.*) Nothing! He attaches—oh! Heavens! You ought to know it!—importance to nothing!

ROXANE (*quickly*). Perhaps he doubted what I said just now? I saw that he doubted it!

CYRANO (*taking her hand*). But did you really tell the truth?

ROXANE. Yes, yes, I should love him even—

(*She hesitates a second.*)

CYRANO (*smiling sadly*). The words will not come before me?

ROXANE. But—

CYRANO. It will not pain me! Even if he were ugly?

ROXANE. Even if he were ugly! (*Firing outside.*) Ah! wait, they are firing!

CYRANO (*ardently*). Even frightful?

ROXANE. Frightful!

CYRANO. Disfigured?

ROXANE. Disfigured!

CYRANO. Grotesque?

ROXANE. Nothing could make him grotesque to me.

CYRANO. You would still love him?

ROXANE. And even more!

CYRANO (*losing his self-control, aside*). My God, perhaps it

is true, and happiness is for me. (*To Roxane.*) I—Roxane—
listen!

LE BRET (*entering hurriedly, calls in a low voice*). Cyrano!

CYRANO (*turning around*). What?

LE BRET. Hush!

(*He speaks to him very low.*)

CYRANO (*dropping Roxane's hand, with a cry*). Oh!

ROXANE. What is the matter?

CYRANO (*to himself, stupefied*). It's all over.

(*New reports.*)

ROXANE. What? What is it? Are they firing?

(*She goes back to look outside.*)

CYRANO. It is all over; never can I tell her now!

ROXANE (*trying to dart forward*). What is going on?

CYRANO (*quickly, stopping her*). Nothing!

(*Cadets enter, concealing something they are carrying, and
they form a group preventing* ROXANE *from coming near.*)

CYRANO (*drawing her away*). Never mind them!

ROXANE. But what were you going to say to me before?

CYRANO. What was I going to say to you?—nothing, oh!
nothing, I assure you, madame! (*Solemnly.*) I swear that
Christian's mind, his soul were—(*correcting himself in alarm*)
—are the greatest—

ROXANE. Were? (*With a scream.*) Ah!

(*She rushes forward and pushes every one aside.*)

CYRANO. It is all over!

ROXANE (*sees Christian lying wrapped in his cloak*). Christian!

LE BRET (*to Cyrano*). The enemy's first shot!

(ROXANE *throws herself on* CHRISTIAN's *body. Renewed firing.
Clashing. Uproar. Drums.*)

CARBON DE CASTEL-JALOUX (*sword in hand*). It is the attack!
To arms!

(*Followed by the* Cadets, *he passes to the other side of the
talus.*)

ROXANE. Christian!

CARBON'S VOICE (*behind the talus*). Make haste!

ROXANE. Christian!

CARBON. *Fall into line!*

ROXANE. Christian!

CARBON. *Look to—your fuse!*

(RAGUENEAU *comes running with water in a helmet.*)

CHRISTIAN (*in a dying voice*). Roxane!

CYRANO (*quickly, and low, in Christian's ear, while Roxane, beside herself, dips a piece of linen, torn from her bosom, in the water, to dress his wound*). I have told her all! She still loves you!

(CHRISTIAN *closes his eyes.*)

ROXANE. What is it, my love?

CARBON. Draw ramrods!

ROXANE (*to Cyrano*). He is not dead?

CARBON. Open the charges with your teeth!

ROXANE. I feel his cheek grow cold against my own!

CARBON. Aim!

ROXANE. A letter on him! (*She opens it.*) For me!

CYRANO (*aside*). My letter!

CARBON. Fire!

(*Firing. Shouts. Noise of battle.*)

CYRANO (*trying to release his hand, which Roxane holds as she kneels*). But, Roxane, they are fighting!

ROXANE (*detaining him*). Stay a little longer. He is dead. You were the only one who knew him. (*She weeps gently.*) Wasn't he an exquisite, a marvellous being?

CYRANO (*standing with head uncovered*). Yes, Roxane.

ROXANE. An unexampled, adorable poet?

CYRANO. Yes, Roxane.

ROXANE. A sublime mind?

CYRANO. Yes, Roxane!

ROXANE. A deep soul, a stranger, unappreciated by the vulgar herd, a magnificent and charming spirit?

CYRANO (*decidedly*). Yes, Roxane!

ROXANE (*throwing herself on Christian's body*). He is dead!

CYRANO (*aside, drawing his sword*). There is nothing for me but to die now! for, without knowing it, she is mourning for me in him!

(*Trumpets in the distance.*)

DE GUICHE (*appearing on the talus, his head bare, wounded in the forehead, in a thundering voice*). 'Tis the promised signal! The flourish of brasses! The French are entering the camp with provisions. Hold out a little longer!

ROXANE. Blood and tears on his letter!

A VOICE (*outside, shouting*). Surrender!

THE CADETS. Never!

RAGUENEAU (*who, having climbed up on his carriage, is watching the battle from above the talus*). The danger is increasing!

CYRANO (*to De Guiche, pointing to Roxane*). Take her away! I am going to take part!

ROXANE (*kissing the letter, in a feeble voice*). His blood! his tears!

RAGUENEAU (*leaping down from the coach to hasten to her*). She is fainting!

DE GUICHE (*on the talus, to the Cadets, furiously*). Hold your ground!

A VOICE (*outside*). Throw down your arms!

CADETS' VOICES. Never!

CYRANO (*to De Guiche*). You have proved your valor, sir: (*pointing to Roxane*) escape with her!

DE GUICHE (*running to Roxane, and lifting her in his arms*). I will! But the victory is ours if you save time!

CYRANO. That is good! (*Calling to Roxane, whom De Guiche, assisted by Ragueneau, is carrying away unconscious.*) Farewell, Roxane!

(*Tumult. Screams.* Cadets *appear wounded, and fall on the stage.* CYRANO, *rushing to the combat, is stopped on the top of the talus by* CARBON DE CASTEL-JALOUX, *covered with blood.*)

CARBON. We are giving way! I have been wounded twice with the halberd!

CYRANO (*shouting to the Gascons*). Courage! Don't give up, boys! (*To Carbon, whom he supports.*) Have no fear! I have two deaths to avenge: Christian's and my own happiness! (*They descend. Cyrano brandishes the lance to which Roxane's handkerchief is fastened.*) Float, little lace flag, bearing her monogram! (*He plants it in the ground; he shouts to the Cadets.*) Fall on them! Crush them! (*To the Fifer.*) A tune on your fife!

(*The* Fifer *plays. The wounded men rise. Some* Cadets, *rolling down the talus, collect around* CYRANO *and the little flag. The coach is covered and filled with men, bristles with arquebuses, and is transformed into a redoubt.*)

A CADET (*appearing on the top of the talus, retreating, but fighting all the while, shouts*): They are coming up the talus (*and drops dead*)!

CYRANO. We will give them a salute!

(*The talus is covered in an instant with a terrible array of the enemy. The grand standards of the Imperials are raised.*)

CYRANO. Fire!

(*General discharge.*)

SHOUT (*in the enemy's ranks*). Fire!

(*Deadly response. The* Cadets *fall on every side.*)

A SPANISH OFFICER (*uncovering*). Who are these men, getting themselves all killed?

CYRANO (*reciting, standing in the midst of the bullets*).

      Ce sont les cadets de Gascogne
      De Carbon de Castel-Jaloux;
      Bretteurs et menteurs sans vergogne.

(*He rushes forward by the survivors.*)

      Ce sont les cadets—

(*The rest is lost in the battle. Curtain falls.*)

ACT FIFTH

Cyrano's Gazette

Fifteen years later, in 1655. The park belonging to the convent occupied by the Sisters *of the Cross, in Paris. Splendid shade trees. On the left, the house; wide steps upon which open several doors. In the middle of the stage, an enormous tree, standing alone in a small oval. In the right foreground, among large box trees a semicircular stone seat.*

A walk shaded by chestnut trees crosses the rear of the stage, and leads on the right background to the door of a chapel partially seen through the branches. Through the double curtain of the trees, are seen glimpses of grass-plots, other walks, thickets, glades of the park, the sky.

A small side door in the chapel opens on a colonnade, entwined with a reddening vine, which is lost to sight on the right foreground, behind the box trees.

It is autumn. All the foliage above the fresh grass is turning red. The box trees and yews form spots of green. Yellow leaves under each tree. Leaves are strewn over the whole stage, crackle under the feet in the walks, half cover the steps and seats.

Between the seat on the right and the tree, a large embroidery frame, in front of which a small chair has been placed. Baskets filled with skeins and balls. Piece of work begun.

As the curtain rises, Sisters *are coming and going in the park: some are seated on the bench around an older nun. Leaves are falling.*

∽∾∽∾∽∾∽∾∽∾∽∾∽∾∽∾∽∾∽∾∽∾∽∾∽∾∽∾∽∾∽∾∽∾∽∾∽

SCENE FIRST

MOTHER MARGUÉRITE, SISTER MARTHE, SISTER CLAIRE, *other* Sisters

SISTER MARTHE (*to Mother Marguérite*). Sister Claire has looked in the glass twice to see how her cap suits her.

MOTHER MARGUÉRITE (*to Sister Claire*). It is very ugly.

SISTER CLAIRE. But Sister Marthe took a plum out of the tart this morning. I saw her.

MOTHER MARGUÉRITE (*to Sister Marthe*). That was very naughty, Sister Marthe.

SISTER CLAIRE. 'Twas only a little glance!

SISTER MARTHE. 'Twas only a little plum!

MOTHER MARGUÉRITE. I shall tell Monsieur Cyrano, this evening.

SISTER CLAIRE (*alarmed*). No! He would laugh at me!

SISTER MARTHE. He will say that nuns are very coquettish!

SISTER CLAIRE. Very greedy!

MOTHER MARGUÉRITE (*smiling*). And very good.

SISTER CLAIRE. Hasn't he been here every Saturday for ten years, Mother Marguérite de Jésus?

MOTHER MARGUÉRITE. And longer! ever since his cousin mingled the worldly mourning of her crêpe veil with our linen caps, and came to settle among us, fourteen years ago, like a great black bird among our white ones!

SISTER MARTHE. He alone, since she came to live in this cloister, has been able to drive away the grief that will not abate.

ALL THE SISTERS. He is so droll!—It is amusing when he comes!—He teases us!—He is nice!—We like him very much! —We make pâte d'angélique for him!

SISTER MARTHE. But, after all, he is not a very good Catholic!

SISTER CLAIRE. We are going to convert him.

THE SISTERS. Yes! yes!

MOTHER MARGUÉRITE. I forbid you to attempt anything of the sort, my children. Do not torment him: perhaps he would not come so often!

SISTER MARTHE. But—Heavens!—

MOTHER MARGUÉRITE. Never fear: God must know him well.

SISTER MARTHE. Every Saturday, when he comes, looking so proud, he says to me as he enters, "My sister, I ate meat yesterday!"

MOTHER MARGUÉRITE. Ah! Does he tell you that? Well! the last time he had eaten nothing for two days.

SISTER MARTHE. My Mother!

MOTHER MARGUÉRITE. He is poor.

SISTER MARTHE. Who told you so?

MOTHER MARGUÉRITE. Monsieur le Bret.

SISTER MARTHE. Doesn't any one assist him?

MOTHER MARGUÉRITE. No, he would be offended.

(*Roxane, dressed in black, with widow's cap and long veil, is seen to appear in one of the walks at the back of the stage; De Guiche, magnificent, but growing old, is beside her. They walk slowly. Mother Marguérite rises.*) Come, we must go in. —Madame Magdeleine is walking in the park with a visitor.

SISTER MARTHE (*in a low voice to Sister Claire*). Is it the Duc de Grammont?

SISTER CLAIRE (*looking*). Yes, I think so.

SISTER MARTHE. He hasn't been to see her for months!

THE SISTERS. He is very much occupied!—With the court!— The camp!

SISTER CLAIRE. The cares of the world!

(*They go out.* DE GUICHE *and* ROXANE *come forward in silence, and stop near the embroidery frame. A pause.*)

SCENE SECOND

ROXANE, *the* DUC DE GRAMMONT, *formerly* COUNT DE GUICHE, *then* LE BRET *and* RAGUENEAU

THE DUKE. Are you going to waste your fairness here forever in mourning?

ROXANE. Forever.

DE GUICHE. Always faithful?

ROXANE. Always.

THE DUKE (*after a time*). You have forgiven me?

ROXANE. Since I am here.

(*New silence.*)

THE DUKE. What a being he was!

ROXANE. You should have known him!

THE DUKE. Ah! I should? I knew him too little, perhaps. His last letter is still next your heart?

ROXANE. Like a sweet scapulary, it hangs from this velvet.

THE DUKE. Though dead, you still love him?

ROXANE. Sometimes it seems to me that he is only half dead, that our hearts are together, and that his love, still alive, is hovering around me!

THE DUKE (*after another silence*). Does Cyrano come to see you?

ROXANE. Yes, often. That old friend takes the place of the newspapers for me. He comes regularly: his chair is placed under the tree where you are, if it is fine; I wait for him with my embroidery; on the last strike of the hour I hear—for I do not even turn my head!—his cane upon the steps; he sits down; he laughs at my everlasting embroidery; he tells me the events of the week, and— (*Le Bret appears on the steps.*) There is Le Bret! (*Le Bret comes down.*) How is our friend?

LE BRET. He is ill.

THE DUKE. Oh!

ROXANE (*to the Duke*). He exaggerates!

LE BRET. Everything is as I predicted: the neglect, the poverty! His letters have made new enemies for him! He attacks the sham nobles, the devotees, the braggarts, plagiarists—every one.

ROXANE. But his sword inspires the deepest fear. No one will ever get the better of him.

THE DUKE (*shaking his head*). Who knows?

LE BRET. What I fear is not these attacks, it is solitude, hunger, it is December entering with wolflike steps into his obscure chamber: these are the assassins that will kill him! Every day he takes in his belt by a notch. His poor nose has taken on the tones of old ivory. He has nothing left but a black serge coat.

THE DUKE. Ah! It hasn't come to that!—Very well, do not pity him too much.

LE BRET (*with a bitter smile*). My lord!

THE DUKE. Do not pity him too much: he has lived without binding himself, free in thought as well as action.

LE BRET (*with a bitter smile*). Your grace!

THE DUKE (*haughtily*). I know, yes: I have everything; he has nothing. But I would very gladly press his hand. (*Bowing to Roxane.*) Farewell.

ROXANE. I will accompany you.

(*The* Duke *bows to* LE BRET *and goes with* ROXANE *toward the steps.*)

THE DUKE (*stopping, while she goes up the steps*). Yes, sometimes I envy him. You see, when one has had too much success in life, one feels—although he has done nothing really wrong—a thousand little dissatisfactions, the sum total of which does not amount to remorse but a vague uneasiness; and a duke's fur-trimmed robes, while mounting the steps of greatness, drag after them the noise of dry illusions and regrets, just as your mourning gown drags the dead leaves as you mount slowly toward these doors.

ROXANE (*sarcastically*). Are you such a dreamer?

THE DUKE. Ah! Yes! (*Just as he is going out, abruptly.*) Monsieur Le Bret! (*To Roxane.*) Will you allow me to speak just a word? (*Goes to Le Bret, and in a low voice.*) It is true: no one would dare attack your friend; but many hate him; and some one said to me yesterday, while playing at the Queen's: "That Cyrano may die by some accident."

LE BRET. Ah!

THE DUKE. Yes. Let him go out little. Let him be cautious.

LE BRET (*lifting his arms in the air*). Cautious! He is going to come here? I must warn him. Yes, but!—

ROXANE (*who has remained on the steps, to one of the Sisters coming toward her*). What is it?

THE SISTER. Ragueneau wishes to see you, madame.

ROXANE. Let him come in. (*To the Duke and to Le Bret.*) He has come to cry poverty. Having set out to be an author, he has gradually become a poet—

LE BRET. A bagnio-keeper—

ROXANE. Actor—

LE BRET. Beadle—

ROXANE. Wig-maker—

LE BRET. Master of the lute—

ROXANE. What can he be to-day?

RAGUENEAU (*entering hurriedly*). Ah! Madame! (*He sees Le Bret.*) Monsieur!

ROXANE (*smiling*). Tell your misfortunes to Let Bret. I am coming back.

RAGUENEAU. But, madame—

(ROXANE *goes out, without listening, with the* Duke. *He comes forward toward* LE BRET.)

SCENE THIRD

LE BRET, RAGUENEAU

RAGUENEAU. Well, since you are here, I would rather not have her know about it! I was going to see your friend just now. I was about twenty steps from his house—when I saw him come out. I am about to join him. He is going to turn the corner of the street—and I run—when from a window, under which he is passing—is it chance?—possibly!—a lackey drops a piece of wood.

LE BRET. The rascal! Cyrano!

RAGUENEAU. I reach him and I see him—

LE BRET. It is frightful!

RAGUENEAU. Our friend, sir, our poet, I see him there on the ground, with a great hole in his head.

LE BRET. Is he dead?

RAGUENEAU. No! but—Heavens! I brought him home to his room. Ah! his room! You ought to see the place!

LE BRET. Is he suffering?

RAGUENEAU. No, sir, he is unconscious.

LE BRET. Did you call a doctor?

RAGUENEAU. One came out of kindness.

LE BRET. My poor Cyrano! Break it gently to Roxane! What does the doctor say?

RAGUENEAU. He spoke—I know no more—of fever, of the brain! Oh, if you should see him—with his head bandaged! Let us go to him at once! There is no one by his bedside! He might die, sir, if he should get up!

LE BRET (*leading him to the right*). Let us go this way! Come, it is shorter! past the chapel!

ROXANE (*appearing on the steps and seeing Le Bret pass through the colonnade leading to the little door in the chapel*). Monsieur le Bret! (*Le Bret and Ragueneau hasten away without replying.*) Does Le Bret go away when he is called? It is some new story of that good Ragueneau's!

(*She comes down the steps.*)

SCENE FOURTH

ROXANE *alone, then two* Sisters *for a moment*

ROXANE. Ah! How beautiful is this last day of September! My sadness smiles. She whom April enshrouded in gloom, finds autumn more in sympathy. (*She sits down by her embroidery frame. Two Sisters come out from the house and bring a large arm-chair under the tree.*) Ah! here is the classic arm-chair in which my old friend comes to sit!

SISTER MARTHE. But it is the best in the parlor!

ROXANE. Thank you, sister. (*The Sisters move away.*) He is coming. (*She settles herself. The clock is heard striking.*) There—the clock is striking!—my worsteds!—The clock has struck? I am surprised! Will he be late for the first time? The sister at the turning-box must be—my thimble?—there, I see it!—exhorting him to penitence. (*A pause.*) She is exhorting him! He cannot be much longer.—Wait! a dead leaf! (*She brushes away the leaf fallen on her frame.*) Besides nothing could—my scissors?—in my bag!—prevent his coming!

A SISTER (*appearing on the steps*). Monsieur de Bergerac.

SCENE FIFTH

ROXANE, CYRANO, *and, for a moment,* SISTER MARTHE

ROXANE (*without turning around*). What was I saying? (*She embroiders. Cyrano, very pale, his hat pulled down over his eyes, appears. The Sister who has announced him enters. He begins to descend the steps slowly with a visible effort to keep from falling, and leaning on his cane. Roxane works at her embroidery.*) Oh! these faded shades. How shall I match them? (*To Cyrano, in a tone of friendly reproach.*) Late for the first time in fourteen years!

CYRANO (*who has reached the arm-chair and seated himself, in a gay voice contrasting with his face*). Yes, it is provoking! I am vexed. I was delayed, confound it!

ROXANE. By?

CYRANO. By a visit which was very inopportune.

ROXANE (*absent-mindedly, working*). Ah! Yes! some disagreeable person.

CYRANO. Yes, cousin, a disagreeable person.

ROXANE. Did you send him away?

CYRANO. Yes. I said: "Excuse me, but this is Saturday, a day when I have to visit a certain house; nothing will prevent me: return in an hour!"

ROXANE (*lightly*). Well! this person will have to wait to see you: I shall not let you go away before evening.

CYRANO. Perhaps I shall have to go a little sooner.

(*He closes his eyes, and does not speak for a moment.* SISTER MARTHE *crosses the park from the chapel to the steps.* ROXANE *sees her, and nods to her.*)

ROXANE (*to Cyrano*). You are not teasing Sister Marthe?

CYRANO (*quickly opening his eyes*). Yes! (*With a comical deep voice.*) Sister Marthe! Come here! (*The Sister approaches him.*) Ha! ha! ha! Those lovely eyes always cast down!

SISTER MARTHE (*lifting her eyes with a smile*). But— (*She notices his face and makes a gesture of surprise.*) Oh!

CYRANO (*in a low voice, pointing to Roxane*). Hush! It is nothing— (*In a blustering voice, aloud.*) Yesterday, I ate meat.

SISTER MARTHE. I know it. (*Aside.*) That is why he is so pale! (*Quickly, and in a low voice.*) If you will come to the refectory by and by, I will make you drink a big bowl of soup. Will you come?

CYRANO. Yes, yes, yes.

SISTER MARTHE. Ah! You are quite reasonable, to-day!

ROXANE (*hearing them whisper*). Is she trying to convert you?

SISTER MARTHE. God forbid!

CYRANO. That is true! You, who are always chattering so

piously, you are not preaching to me? It is surprising, indeed! (*With mock fury.*) Ye gods and little fishes! I should like to surprise you too! Wait, I will allow you— (*He appears to be looking for a good way to tease her, and to find it.*) Ah! A new idea!—to—to pray for me, to-night, in church.

ROXANE. Oh! oh!

CYRANO (*laughing*). Sister Marthe is stupefied.

SISTER MARTHE (*softly*). I did not wait for your permission. (*She goes away again.*)

CYRANO (*coming back to Roxane, leaning on her embroidery frame*). Ye powers, I shall never see the end of this embroidery!

ROXANE. I was expecting that jest.

(*At this moment, a slight breeze causes the leaves to fall.*)

CYRANO. The leaves!

ROXANE (*raising her head, and looking toward the paths in the distance*). They are Venetian yellow. Watch them fall.

CYRANO. How well they fall! In this short journey from the branch to the earth, they succeed in showing a final beauty, and, in spite of their fear of rotting on the ground, desire this fall to assume the grace of flight!

ROXANE. Are you melancholy?

CYRANO (*recovering himself*). Not at all, Roxane!

ROXANE. Well, let the leaves fall from the plane tree—and tell me the news. Where is my gazette?

CYRANO. Here it is!

ROXANE. Ah!

CYRANO (*growing paler and paler, and struggling against the pain*). Saturday, the nineteenth: the King, having eaten grape-jam for the eighth time, was seized with a fever; he was bled twice and his malady condemned for high treason, and now his august pulse resumes its normal beat. At the Queen's grand ball, Sunday, they burned seven hundred and sixty-three white wax candles; they say that our troops have beaten John of Austria; four witches have been hung; the little dog belonging to Madame d'Athis had to take a clyster—

ROXANE. Monsieur de Bergerac, will you be still!

CYRANO. Monday—nothing. Lygdamire changed her lover.

ROXANE. Oh!

CYRANO (*whose face changes more and more*). Tuesday, the entire court was at Fontainebleau. Wednesday, La Montglat said, "No!" to the Count de Fiesque. Thursday: Mancini was queen of France—or almost! The twenty-fifth, La Montglat said, "Yes," to De Fiesque; and Saturday, the twenty-sixth—

(*He closes his eyes. His head drops forward. Silence.*)

ROXANE (*surprised at not hearing more, turns around, looks at him, and rises frightened*). Has he fainted? (*She runs toward him, crying out:*) Cyrano!

CYRANO (*opening his eyes again, in an indistinct voice*). What is it? What? (*He sees Roxane bending over him, and quickly settling his hat on his head, draws back frightened into his chair.*) No! No! I assure you, it is nothing. Let me be!

ROXANE. But—

CYRANO. It is the wound I received at Arras—that—sometimes—you know—

ROXANE. My poor friend!

CYRANO. But it is nothing. It will pass away. (*He smiles with an effort.*) It is gone.

ROXANE (*standing near him*). Each of us has a wound: I have mine. That old wound, always fresh, is still there (*she puts her hand on her breast*), it is there, under the letter with its paper now grown yellow, on which can still be seen the tears and the blood!

(*Twilight begins to come on.*)

CYRANO. His letter! Did you not tell me that some day, perhaps, you would let me read it?

ROXANE. Ah! Would you like to read his letter?

CYRANO. Yes. I desire it—to-day—

ROXANE (*giving him the little bag hanging from her neck*). Take it!

CYRANO (*taking it*). May I open it?

ROXANE. Open it—read it!

(*She returns to her frame, folds it up, arranges her worsteds.*)

CYRANO (*reading*). "Roxane, farewell, I am going to die!—"

ROXANE (*stopping, surprised*). Aloud?

CYRANO (*reading*). "I believe it will be to-night, my dearly beloved! My soul is still heavy with unspoken love, and I am dying! Never again, never shall my infatuated eyes,—"

ROXANE. How you read his letter!

CYRANO (*continuing*). "My looks thrilled by the feast, embrace your graceful, airy gestures; I recall a little one peculiarly your own, of touching your forehead, and I would cry out—"

ROXANE. How you read that letter!

(*Darkness falls insensibly.*)

CYRANO. "And I cry out: 'Farewell!' "

ROXANE. You read it . . .

CYRANO. "My dear, my dearest, my treasure" . . .

ROXANE. In a voice . . .

CYRANO. "My love!" . . .

ROXANE. In a voice—why—that I do not hear for the first time!

(*She approaches very softly, without his noticing her, passes behind the arm-chair, bends over noiselessly, and looks at the letter. The darkness increases.*)

CYRANO. "My heart has never left you for a second, and I am and shall be even in the other world the one whose love for you is without measure, who" . . .

ROXANE (*places her hand on his shoulder*). How can you read now? It is dark. (*He starts, turns around, sees her very near him, makes a gesture of alarm, bends his head. A long silence. Then, in the darkness, which has grown complete, she says slowly, joining her hands:*) And for fourteen years, he has played this rôle, of being the old friend come to amuse me!

CYRANO. Roxane!

ROXANE. It was you!

CYRANO. No, no, Roxane, no!

ROXANE. I ought to have guessed it when he spoke my name!

CYRANO. No! it was not I!

ROXANE. It was you!

CYRANO. I swear to you . . .

ROXANE. I see through all your generous imposture: the letters were yours . . .

CYRANO. No!

ROXANE. The words so madly fond, it was you . . .

CYRANO. No.

ROXANE. The voice in the darkness was yours!

CYRANO. I swear to you that it was not!

ROXANE. The soul was yours!

CYRANO. I did not love you!

ROXANE. You loved me!

CYRANO. It was another!

ROXANE. You loved me!

CYRANO. No!

ROXANE. Already you say it lower!

CYRANO. No, no, my dear love, I loved you not!

ROXANE. Ah! How many things are dead, how many things are born! Why have you kept silent these fourteen years, since on this letter which was nothing to him, these tears are yours?

CYRANO (*handing her the letter*). The blood was his.

ROXANE. Then why let this sublime silence be broken to-day?

CYRANO. Why?

(LE BRET *and* RAGUENEAU *come running in*.)

SCENE SIXTH

The Same, LE BRET, *and* RAGUENEAU

LE BRET. What imprudence! Ah! I was sure of it! He is there!

CYRANO (*smiling and straightening himself up*). Heavens!

LE BRET. He has killed himself, madame, by getting up!

ROXANE. Great God! Just now—this weakness? this?

CYRANO. Very true! I had not finished my gazette: on Saturday, the twenty-sixth, an hour before dinner, Monsieur de Bergerac received his death-blow.

(*He takes off his hat; they see the linen bandages on his head.*)

ROXANE. What does he say?—Cyrano!—His head bandaged! —Oh, what have they done to you? Why?

CYRANO. "Slain by a hero, to fall with the sword-point in my heart!" Yes, I said that! Fate is a mocker! And here I am killed, entrapped, from behind, by a lackey, hit by a block of wood! This is very good. I shall have failed in everything, even my death.

RAGUENEAU. Ah! My dear sir!

CYRANO. Ragueneau, do not weep so! (*He holds out his hand to him.*) What have you become now, my brother?

RAGUENEAU (*through his tears*). I am candle—candle-snuffer, for Molière.

CYRANO. Molière!

RAGUENEAU. But I am going to leave him after to-morrow; yes, I am indignant! Yesterday, they played "Scapin," and I saw that he had taken the scene from you!

LE BRET. The entire scene!

RAGUENEAU. Yes, sir, the famous "What the devil is he going to do?"

LE BRET. Molière took it from you!

CYRANO. Hush! hush! He did well! (*To Ragueneau.*) The scene produced a good effect, did it not?

RAGUENEAU (*sobbing*). Ah! sir, the people laughed and laughed!

CYRANO. Yes, my life has been to prompt others—and be forgotten! (*To Roxane.*) Do you remember the night when Christian spoke to you under the balcony? Well! my whole life is there: while I remained below in the black darkness, others climbed to win the kiss of glory! It is justice and I admit, on the threshold of the tomb, that Molière has genius and Christian had beauty! (*At this moment, the bells in the chapel having sounded, the Nuns are seen passing along the walk in the background, on their way to service.*) Let them go to prayers, since their bell has rung!

ROXANE (*rising to call one of them*). My sister! my sister!

CYRANO (*detaining her*). No! no! Do not go for any one: when you returned, I should be no longer here. (*The Nuns have entered the chapel; the organ is heard.*) I felt the need of a little harmony—there it is.

ROXANE. I love you; you must live!

CYRANO. No! for in the fairy tale, when she says, "I love you," the prince, filled with shame, feels his ugliness melt away in the sunshine of these words—but you would see that I remained the same.

ROXANE. I have been the cause of your misfortune! I have! I have!

CYRANO. You? On the contrary! I knew nothing of feminine sweetness. My mother never thought me handsome. I had no sister. Later on I dreaded the mocking eye of a sweetheart. I owe it to you for having had at least a friend. Thanks to you, a woman's gown has entered into my life.

LE BRET (*pointing to the moonlight coming through the branches*). Your other friend has come to see you!

CYRANO (*smiling to the moon*). I see her.

ROXANE. I loved but one single being, and I must lose him twice!

CYRANO. Le Bret, I am going to climb to the opaline moon to-day, without inventing any machine—

ROXANE. What are you saying?

CYRANO. Yes, 'tis there, I tell you, that they will send me for my paradise. More than one soul I love must be exiled there, and I shall find Socrates and Galileo!

LE BRET (*rebelling*). No! no! The end is too stupid and too unjust! Such a poet! A soul so large and lofty! To die like this! To die!

CYRANO. There is Le Bret grumbling again!

LE BRET (*bursting into tears*). My dear friend—

CYRANO (*rising, with a wild look on his face*). Ce sont les cadets de Gascogne— The elementary mass— Ah! yes!—there is the "hic"—

LE BRET. His science—even in his delirium!

CYRANO. Copernicus said—

ROXANE. Oh!

CYRANO. But what the devil was he going to do, but what business had he there?

> Philosopher, physician,
> Rhymer, swordsman, musician,
> And aerial traveller,
> Great in fencing,
> A lover too—to his sorrow—
> Here lies Hercule-Savinien
> De Cyrano de Bergerac.

But pardon me, I am going away, I cannot cause delay: you see the moonlight has come to take me: (*He falls back in his chair, Roxane's tears bring him back to reality, he looks at her and caresses her veil.*) I do not care to have you grieve less for that charming, good, handsome Christian; but when the great cold shall have seized my members, I simply wish that you would give a double meaning to this veil, and that you may wear your mourning a little for me as well as him.

ROXANE. I promise you!

CYRANO (*is seized with great shivering, and suddenly rises*). Not there! no! not in that arm-chair! (*They rush toward him.*) Do not support me! Do not! (*He leans against the tree.*) Nothing but the tree! (*Silence.*) He is coming. I already feel shod with marble,—gloved with lead! (*He grows stiff.*) Oh! but!—since he is on the way, I will await him standing (*he draws his sword*),—sword in hand!

LE BRET. Cyrano!

ROXANE (*in a faltering voice*). Cyrano!

(*All draw back terrified.*)

CYRANO. I believe that he is looking, that he dares to look at my nose, the noseless one! (*He lifts his sword.*) What do you say? It is useless! I know it! But one does not fight with hope of success! No! no! It is a much finer thing when it is useless! What are all those? Are you a thousand? Ah! I recognize you, all my old enemies! Lying? (*He strikes the air with his sword.*) Wait, wait! Ha! ha! the Compromises, Prejudices, Cowardice! (*He strikes.*) Shall I make a compact? Never, never! Ah! There you are too, Folly! I know that at last you will put me down; no matter: I fight! I fight! I fight! (*Makes wide circles in the air with his sword, and stops, panting for breath.*) Yes, you have torn everything from me, the laurel and the rose! Take them! In spite of you, there is one thing I shall take with me, and to-night, when I enter God's house, my salutation shall sweep the blue threshold, with something free from creases, free from stain, which I shall carry in spite of you (*he raises the sword high*),—and that is—

(*The sword escapes from his hand, he totters, and falls into the arms of* LE BRET *and* RAGUENEAU.)

ROXANE (*bending over him and kissing his forehead*). That is?

CYRANO (*opens his eyes, recognizes her, and with a smile says*): My plume.

CURTAIN FALLS